The Beast of
ADAM
GORIGHTLY

Collected Rantings (1992-2004)

"The Beast of Adam Gorightly: Collected Rantings (1992-2004)," by Adam Gorightly. ISBN 1-58939-781-9.

Published 2005 by Virtualbookworm.com Publishing Inc., P.O. Box 9949, College Station, TX 77842, US. ©2005, Adam Gorightly. All rights reserved. No part of this publication may be reproduced, stored in a retrieval system, or transmitted in any form or by any means, electronic, mechanical, recording or otherwise, without the prior written permission of Adam Gorightly.

Manufactured in the United States of America.

Faint Praise for Adam Gorightly

"Considering I despise Adam Gorightly as a loathsome excuse for a human being, my advocation of this collection isn't due to any silly, sentimental friendship. Read this book, but stay away from the SOB."
- Robert Sterling, Konformist.com

"Mr. Gorightly's words are like a handful of sun filled pills...or a calgon bath...or a shot of smack...I'm hooked!"
- Shane Bugbee, www.threeringradio.com

"Adam Gorightly fluctuates within the gray matter of our cerebral cortex, spinning and swirling a weave of metaphorical elements and parables as territorial lines between truthful accounts and fictional realms detonate."
- Otis Fodder, www.otisfodder.com

"A crackpot historian of the highest order!"
- Victor Thorn, Wing TV

"Adam is the type of writer who scribbles, then comes into town, insults you, drinks your liquor, hits on your wife and then demands a free room--buyer beware!"
- David Reimer, a former friend

"When Adam Gorightly gets his teeth into something, he goes right down to the bone. No poison, though."
- Louise Lacey, author of
*- **Lunaception: A feminine odyssey into fertility and contraception***

"These experiences have not credibility...because drugs create delusions, nightmares..."
- Jean Sider, French Ufologist

"Adam Gorightly has expertly and consistently navigated the hinterlands of fringe culture and extreme expression, but for some reason doesn't have the balls to use his real name."
-Greg Bishop, The Excluded Middle

The Beast of
ADAM
GORIGHTLY

Collected Rantings (1992-2004)

Contents

Dedicated to the original members
of the Discordian Society

Greg Hill, Kerry Thornley, Bob Newport, Louise Lacey, Robert Anton Wilson and Camden Benares.

Hail Eris! All Hail Discordia!

Credits

Cover art by Ashleigh Talbot, www.madametalbot.com

Cover design by Andrew Taylor, www.taopro.com

Interior artwork on pages 1, 6, 23, 61, 110 by Mack White,
www.mackwhite.com

Interior artwork on pages 25, 81, 87, 176 by Eric York, Global Maggot
Productions

Intro

Friends, you hold before you now twelve years of toil and folly, a collection of my best (and worst!) articles, published and some previously unpublished from the years 1992 through 2004.

"The Disneyland Dead" originally appeared in *INFOCULT* magazine, and later on the Internet at *Babel Magazine.*

"*Is The Catcher in the Rye* a Mechanism of Control?" originally appeared in *Paranoia: The Conspiracy Reader*, and was later reprinted in *Quimby's Queer Store* magazine and on the Internet at wingtv.net

"A Trip To The Mound With Dock Ellis" and "The Trickster of Truths" appeared in *Wake Up Down There: The Excluded Middle Anthology*, edited by Greg Bishop.

"Rock and Roll Minions of Satan" originally appeared in Tim Cridland's *Off The Deep End* magazine and later appeared in an alternate version in *Paranoia: The Conspiracy Reader*, PO Box 1041, Providence, RI 02901, www.paranoiamagazine.com

"John Lilly, Ketamine and The Entities From ECCO" originally appeared in *Crash Collusion* magazine, and later resurfaced at Conspiracyarchive.com

"Somewhere Over The Rainbow, Man" appeared at Donna Kossy's *Kooks* website and was later reprinted in a re-edited version in *FourTwoFour*, Britain's largest Soccer magazine.

"Jim Keith, Burning Man and Wounded Knee" and "Kerouac's CITYCitycity" originally appeared in *SteamShovel Press* magazine.

"Ritual Magic, Mind Control and the UFO Phenomenon" and "The Montauk Mythos (Part 1)" originally appeared in *Dagobert's Revenge* magazine.

Adam Gorightly

"Excerpt from 'UFO's, LSD and Me'" originally appeared in *Crash Collusion* magazine.

"The Manson Family and the Beatles" and "The Prankster or The Manchurian Candidate? The Strange but True Story of Kerry Thornley" originally appeared in *Paranoia: The Conspiracy Reader*

"Human Stew", "Tales from the Astral Plane", "Twelve Spooky Fingers", and "The Word" originally appeared at *Elf Infested Spaces* online.

"Flowers and Blood" originally appeared in *Babel Magazine* online.

"An Interpretation Of Kubrick's *Eyes Wide Shut*" and "Victory Day Parade" originally appeared at Konformist.com

"Hitler Was A Good American: The Bush Crime Family and a Kinder, Gentler Fascism" originally appeared in *The Bush Junta* edited by Mack White and Gary Groth.

"Conspiratorial Recollections: An Interview With Adam Gorightly" originally appeared at *New World Disorder Magazine* online.

The Disneyland Dead

According to sources inside the Magic Kingdom, there have been 17 deaths in the park since it first opened over 45 years ago. My source--a mid level Disney employee--informs me that only one of these 17 deaths was that of a Disneyland cast member. The other 16 fatalities were those of innocent people visiting the park, looking forward to a day of fun and frolic, and instead finding only death and dismemberment at the hands of Uncle Walt's magical killing machines.

My source, whom I will call "The Conductor", has been employed by the Disney Corporation for just under two years, so his knowledge of all the Disneyland deaths and their subsequent cover-ups is somewhat limited. From "The Conductor"--after plying him with alcohol one night--I garnered knowledge of three of these horrifying deaths, the most infamous being the horrid accident which befell the aforementioned cast member. Her name I have been unable to secure. But to all Disneyland employees aware of her gruesome story, she will be known forever as The Squish Girl.

The Squish Girl was an operator for the now defunct ride "America Sings!" This ride, which is still in operation at Florida's Disney World, featured, among others, characters from the Brer Rabbit story. (These very same characters were removed from the ride after its closure. They can now be found in the most recent addition to Disneyland, Splash Mountain, singing their same insipid song, with the blood of The Squish Girl still upon their animated paws.) For some unknown reason, The Squish Girl did a big unexplained no-no. She stepped off the operator's chair as the ride was going and became horribly entrapped between two moving objects. I guess you can figure out how she got her name. The section of Tomorrowland that housed "America Sings!" is now used exclusively by Disney employees for training and other purposes. Still, mysteriously, The Squish Girl's spirit is said to wander there. Often, in the dead of night, the lights in this building have been know to go off and on for no apparent reason. Some employees say it is The Squish Girl trying to contact them.

But if any attraction in Disneyland is haunted, it would probably be the Matterhorn. Like the ferocious Abominable Snowman it houses within, the Matterhorn has swallowed its victim's whole. And after having devoured their flesh and precious bodily fluids, has spat from it whatever bones and blood that could not be digested.

For anybody who has ever ridden the Matterhorn, it seems as if--as your being propelled through its dark, ominous caverns--your head is barely clearing the rocky walls inside, and you find yourself reflexively ducking as your are sped around treacherous corners on this death-defying roller coaster ride through the mountain. This is, in fact, true, for there is very little clearance between yourself and the walls and overhanging rocks, which you would discover if for some stupid reason you decided to stand up. Unfortunately, some poor soul did just that on one occasion and was instantly decapitated. On another grisly occasion, one of the roller coaster cars broke free of the tracks, and flew hundreds of feet into the air, its hapless occupants plummeting to their untimely deaths in the nearby submarine lagoon.

These are just a few of the Disneyland dead.

Is *The Catcher in the Rye* a Mechanism of Control?

One night not long ago, while dozing off to sleep, I was stirred from hypnogogia by the radio faintly humming by my head. When I heard the name J.D. Salinger my curiosity was immediately aroused and I turned the volume up. It was a brief news item, relating the event of Salinger's home burning down in New Hampshire. The news announcer described how Salinger and his wife had watched the conflagration helplessly from a distance, as the firefighters futilely battled to save their home. Anyway, this was the last I heard of the story, which isn't surprising given the elusive nature of Salinger, dropping from view as he did in 1965 and becoming a recluse.

Curious as to what Salinger had done over the years since his disappearance from the public eye, I chanced upon the biography *In Search of J. D. Salinger* by Ian Hamilton. One area of interest I had was Salinger's connections with U.S. Intelligence. My reason for this line of inquiry stemmed from my suspicion that his classic novel *The Catcher in the Rye* had been used as a "mechanism of control" in the assassination of John Lennon, and the attempted assassination of Ronald Reagan. If you recall, *The Catcher in the Rye* was found in the possession of both Hinkley and Chapman after their respective rampages. In fact, when the New York City police apprehended Chapman in the aftermath of Lennon's assassination, he was sitting glassy-eyed and zombified, leaning against the Dakota Building, reading Salinger's book.

When I refer to *The Catcher in the Rye* as a "mechanism of control" I mean in the sense of a triggering device, which sets off a post-hypnotic suggestion, much like the queen of hearts in Richard Condon's *Manchurian Candidate*, unleashing within its mind-controlled subjects the command to kill. According to Hamilton's biography, Salinger was under the employ of Defense Intelligence during World War II, serving with the Counter Intelligence Corps (CIC), his time spent mainly in the interrogation of captured Nazis. Later on, toward the end of the war, Salinger was involved in the denazification of Germany.

4

Denazification could be construed as a code word alluding to the importation of high-level Nazi spies into the highest ranks of the American Intelligence Community under the auspices of Project Paperclip, the top secret operation--which at the war's end--smuggled hundreds of Nazis out of Germany. These "reformed" Nazis were then given new identities, in time forming the core of the new U.S. intelligence, defense and aerospace establishments.

According to the late conspiracy researcher Mae Brussell, it was this American/Nazi alliance that reformed the old Office of Strategic Services (OSS) into its new and improved Nazi-ised version: the Central Intelligence Agency. Perhaps, in this instance, Re-nazification would have been a more apropos term. From this point of reference, it would take a rather fanciful leap to entertain the notion that Salinger was part of this diabolical plot; and going even further to suggest that under the auspices of this new American/Nazi Intelligence regime he wrote *The Catcher in the Rye* as a "mechanism of control" to be employed in CIA mind-control experiments such as Project Artichoke and MK-Ultra.

Personally, I don't suspect that Salinger was wittingly contracted by U.S. Intelligence to covertly compose *The Catcher in the Rye* for nefarious reasons. However, I do consider it quite possible that *The Catcher in the Rye* has been used as a "mechanism of control." In this same fashion, the music of The Beatles was possibly used, in a similar manner, to not only program Mark David Chapman, but the evil Manson clan, as well. According to Vincent Bugliosi in his best seller *Helter Skelter!*, the Mansonoids used bizarre interpretations of Beatles songs to guide them on their murderous rampages through the Hollywood Hills in the summer of 1969.

Furthermore—according to Mae Brussell and other researchers— the Manson Family was nothing less than a full blown CIA Mind Control experiment designed to cast aspersions on the whole counterculture movement of the late '60s by showing that long hair, free love, rock music and drugs would lead the youth of America into a violent all out war against Mom, Apple Pie and the American Way.

Admittedly, these are tenuous connections, but are nonetheless areas that need to be delved into more deeply, especially when one takes into account the general progression of Nazi importees into the U.S. Intelligence Community, and the subsequent creation of mind control programs which reek of Nazi inspiration and influence. Mind programming seems over and again to rear its hideous head where major political assassinations have occurred. When these similar patterns turn up repeatedly, we are forced to ask ourselves if these are simply mere coincidence, or planned procedures executed to achieve a desired end.

So—going one speculative step further—not only can these "mechanisms of control" be employed in programming minds to kill political leaders and activists. In addition, they can also be used as a method to discredit the likes of Salinger or The Beatles by demonstrating to the world at large that such works of art (*The Catcher in the Rye* and *The White Album*) are dangerous to the minds of our country's youth, ostensibly driving them to madness and murder.

2004-03-23 - *Wireless Flash* Weird News
Conspiracy Theorist Accuses Mel Gibson Of Plagiarism

LOS ANGELES, Calif. (Wireless Flash) -- First, Mel Gibson was accused of anti-Semitism for *The Passion Of The Christ* and now a conspiracy theorist in California is accusing him of plagiarism for his 1997 film, *Conspiracy Theory*.

Adam Gorightly claims the thriller's plot rips off a conspiracy theory he created in 1992 about *The Catcher In The Rye* being used as a "triggering device" for mind-controlled assassins like John Hinckley and Mark David Chapman.

Gorightly created the theory after realizing assassins were both fans of the book and wrote an article for *Paranoia* magazine in 1992.

Although screenwriter Brian Helgeland wrote the script, Gorightly thinks Gibson was involved because "...he was reading all sorts of conspiracy books before the movie was made."

Gorightly is exploring legal options but admits he might be willing to settle with Gibson if the actor buys the film rights for his new book, *The Prankster And The Conspiracy* (Paraview Press), which examines how John F. Kennedy's assassination influenced the 1960s counter-culture.

Tuesday Weld Is Watching You:

The Shocking Truth of Occult Secret Societies in Santa Cruz!

Santa Cruz, California was the venue for my latest adventure in the realms of "Conspiracy Theory" sleuthing. My tour guide for this paradigm shattering experience was Douglas Hawes, a former Santa Cruz resident, who was part of the city's punk music scene in the mid to late '80's. Doug and I specifically planned this outing to discuss certain theories revealed to him over the last decade by a certain mysterious "source" he had mentioned numerous times over the course of a yearlong email correspondence.

I met up with Doug at the town's famous eatery, Zachary's, and over breakfast we swapped tales of mind control conspiracies and UFO high weirdness. After a couple hours of spirited conversation amid a heightened caffeine-fueled state of awareness, Doug suggested that we pay a visit to his aforementioned "source", whom he had made many a reference to throughout the course of our correspondence, which included stunning revelations regarding a worldwide Illuminati conspiracy engineered by none other than 60's screen starlet Tuesday Weld (!). The source of these mind-cracking revelations--Doug informed me--was 49-year-old Jeff Turner, and that being in the presence of this individual, he said half-jokingly, was what he termed "The Jeff Turner Experience". The phenomenon was akin to, Doug went on to say, witnessing The Jimi Hendrix Experience circa '67 behind a hit of Owsley Blue: you leave with a mind fully blown, reeling in the aftermath of said encounter.

Doug first met Jeff Turner in 1987, and soon became privy to Turner's conspiratorial cosmology, which--as previously noted-- revolves in part around sex kitten Tuesday Weld, who, Jeff contends, descended from a royal bloodline of Druid witches, and at a very early age had been selected as high priestess in the international Illuminati hierarchy. From this position of occult authority, Weld was able to wield great control over the 60's counterculture, secretly influencing

8

such luminaries as the Beatles, the Rolling Stones, among other rock groups and movie stars of the era, meanwhile pulling the strings behind world events, exercising her occult influence in the realms of political intrigue.

This was just the tip of a weighty iceberg that Douglas Hawes laid on me as we walked the two blocks of Pacific Avenue to his car. Along the way, Doug bumped into a young man named Jordy, and the two talked briefly about a certain "project" the fellow was working on. After they parted, Doug matter of factly stated that Jordy was among a group of young filmmakers currently producing a documentary chronicling the life of none other than Jeff Turner!

On our drive over to Turner's place--located in the Live Oak section of town--Doug laid the groundwork for our forthcoming meeting by describing Turner as someone who is "well connected" and "in the know"; an insider into the arcane conspiracies and shadowy doings of an occult world to which most of us are totally unaware. For whatever reasons, Jeff has become finely tuned into this shadow world, able to read between the lines and make those conspiratorial connections that elude popular consensus reality.

Yet, on the other hand, this man of mystery and perpetual conspiracies is a societal outcast, inhabiting a low rent hovel and subsisting on SSI disability, mainly due to the difficulty he finds functioning in the work-a-day world. Considered by some an unemployable mooch bilking the system, Turner isn't overly concerned with clean clothes, tidy living quarters or people's opinions of him. A certifiable slob, Jeff is unimpressed with social status or what you might have to say about those stains on his shirtsleeve; he is in many ways a man "not of this world". And if even a small percentage of what he says is true, then you sure can't blame the guy for not wanting to play the game of getting ahead or climbing some corporate ladder. Perhaps Jeff sees the limitations of "playing the game" and "getting ahead" as shortsighted in terms of the big picture of what's really going on behind the scenes of world events. But I guess washing your clothes or removing that unsightly ring from your toilet bowl is ultimately irrelevant when it comes to exposing satanic cults involved in ritual human sacrifice. Except from the standpoint that you might want to make yourself more presentable or people will tune you out before they even hear the message. Not saying this is right, but it's nonetheless the reality of social interactions, and for this reason Jeff may never be able to reach a large audience with his message, which is hard enough to swallow as it is.

But slob though he may be, Jeff isn't a sloppy thinker. He has a cohesive worldview--however far out it may seem to mainstream America. Jeff possesses an eidetic memory, and a wealth of conspiratorial knowledge that never fails to tie things together in some meaningful fashion. Like his long time friend Douglas Hawes insists, there's a consistency to the strange universe Jeff Turner presents in his rapid fire discourses that could conceivably go on forever, as one subject leads to another and ties back into a convoluted conspiratorial framework, inevitably inspiring the cornered listener (however interested he or she may actually be) to eventually (as the hour grows late) make use of a window of opportunity to ensure a quick getaway before Jeff gets off on another train of thought that will eventually loop back around and converge with the central theme of his life ala Tiffany and the "All Nations Movement". More on that later...

As we three drove over to the Capitola Book Café, Jeff--aware that I had written a book on the Manson Family--immediately informed me that he had actually known Charles Manson! Jeff went on to say that he and Manson had met a number of times, it turns out, after Charlie'd been released from prison in 1967, during the Tuesday Weld/Illuminati inspired conspiracy called "The Summer of Love". When I asked Jeff how he came to meet Manson (was it mere coincidence or something more?) Jeff attributed it all to synchronicity, that perplexing phenomena widely known to conspiracy buffs and Discordians alike, which attempts to explain those unexplainable coincidences, such as how Jeff's path had been interwoven with the likes of Manson, Tuesday Weld, et al, for strange and mysterious reasons.

At first exposure to such extraordinary claims, one's natural reaction is to dismiss them as the ravings of the drug addled or brain damaged. But the fact of the matter is Jeff doesn't drink or use drugs, and is a regular churchgoer. And while his theories might seem a bit daffy, there was nothing that came out of our conversations that led me to suspect he'd made this stuff up, which is not to suggest that many of Jeff's central theories aren't simply colorful extrapolations on known facts, or outright confabulations. As Douglas Hawes explains, "(Jeff's) stories have remained consistent over many years. I have asked him repeated questions, using different angles, about the same subjects, time and time again. And his stories remain consistent." Furthermore, Doug has received independent corroboration for some of Jeff's more controversial claims, which makes it difficult to dismiss him. Whatever the truth of the matter, it certainly isn't all just one big put-on, as it's evident that Jeff is sincere when he talks about the strange world revolving all around him.

Midway through our Capitola Book Café scone repast, Doug got a cell call from the guy filming the documentary about Jeff, Sean Donnelly of Double Chin Productions. Sean informed Doug that he was on his way over to document our meeting of the minds, which by now was beginning to raise the collective eyebrows of the store's staff. Meanwhile, Jeff--oblivious to the curious reactions of those within earshot--continued to hold court amid the comings and goings of the store's puzzled patrons, who, as they passed by and got a snatch of our curious conversation, must have thought we three had earned a day's pass from the local booby hatch, so preposterous sounding was some of the stuff coming from our table.

A few minutes later, Donnelly showed up and started interviewing Jeff about Tuesday Weld and her Illuminati stranglehold on the 60's counterculture. Soon I, as well, had a camera thrust in my face, and was questioned regarding my views on the World According to Jeff. However, this didn't deter Jeff from talking at the same time, and I really wasn't able to get a word in edgewise--not that it really mattered, or that I had anything particularly significant to say. Just the same, it wasn't a total loss: I was able to hawk my latest book *The Prankster and the Conspiracy*, holding it up to the camera like a proud papa. (Available for $16.95 from Paraview Press! Get yours now while supplies last!)

When Jeff and I were left alone for a few minutes--he took the opportunity to explain how he knew about all these secrets of the Illuminati: It's because he *is* the Priory of Sion, the actual Holy Grail, which is another way of saying the second coming of Christ. With this matter of fact utterance, the intense gleam that's always in Jeff's eyes ratcheted up another notch, and I knew at that instant I had entered into…(insert *Twilight Zone* theme here)…THE JEFF TURNER EXPERIENCE! When I later reflected upon this controversial pronouncement, I thought I might've misinterpreted Jeff, and that what he was actually telling me was that he belonged to the royal bloodline of Christ, which is not such a far out notion these days what with the acceptance of such books as *Holy Blood, Holy Grail*. Whatever the case, my head was starting to hurt.

As it turns out, Jeff Turner's seemingly bizarre conspiratorial cosmology has a local flavor, involving a former Santa Cruzan, whose name shall go unwritten for obvious legal reasons. We'll simply refer to her as the abbreviated "K.M."

According to Jeff, K.M.--as an adolescent in the late 1960's--purportedly got involved in satanic circles in the South Bay, and soon became a protégé of Tuesday Weld. Over time, K.M. built an occult crime club around herself and, in 1974, assumed control of the notorious Process Church of the Final Judgment, a satanic organization allegedly linked to the Manson Family and the Son of Sam killings.

In time, the Weld/K.M. alliance soured and they became bitter enemies. Up until 1991, the two engaged in an ongoing war carried out by K.M.'s supporters and the opposing Weldian faction. Concurrently, K.M. cultivated a powerful satanic cult--with ties to the World Nazi Network--conducting a virtual a reign of terror throughout Santa Cruz and Santa Clara counties.

As Douglas Hawes explained, "Back in 1986-88 Santa Cruz was a whirlpool of weird psychic energies. Anton LaVey was rumored to be living in a house on Wharf Road in Capitola. Tuesday Weld and her archrival K.M. were waging a behind-the-scenes occult war for supremacy in the city...

"Santa Cruz was considered in the eighties by New Age circles to be the great "power point" of spiritual transformation for the whole world. This power point, according to one of my sources, had left Shambhala in the Gobi Desert in the sixties or seventies, was now over Santa Cruz...So occultic circles, aware of this fact, were battling for control of the city...

"There is no public knowledge of K.M.'s involvement in the Process Church. A four and a half year-long investigation by the Santa Clara County District Attorney into her activities was never made public because an indictment was never issued. So she has received absolutely no publicity of any kind...The Federal government has some kind of ongoing investigation into K.M.'s activities. My hunch is that the Feds realize that she knows too much, has compromised too many powerful people, and so could not be taken down without exacting a terrible toll." Meanwhile, according to Doug, K.M. has promoted the public image of a concerned community activist with important connections and influence in political circles, who remain unaware of her occult and criminal activities.

As synchronicity would have it, Jeff Turner was a contemporary of K.M., attending the same high school as this wicked high priestess, who, Jeff asserts, has been involved in child sacrifice rituals. Due to this dangerous knowledge, and his opposition to K.M., Jeff was subsequently persecuted by her satanic henchmen. Several years after graduating from high school, Jeff claims he was approached by the CIA and recruited into their network directed against K.M. More recently, Jeff claims to have provided a sizeable body of materials to former governor George Deukmejian's Special Select Task Force on Satanic Abatement.

Jeff has also been a major player in the West Coast conspiracy scene dating back to the heyday of the Queen Mother of conspiracy research, Mae Brussell, when Jeff was a call-in regular to her Carmel KLRB radio show in the 1980's. In fact, it was Jeff (at least according to Jeff) who led Mae's research into the military's involvement with the occult, satanism and child abductions, knowledge which some suggest ultimately led to Mae's untimely undoing.

In December of 1991 (Jeff went on to inform me) Tuesday Weld stepped down from her lofty perch as the "all seeing eye" of the Illuminati at the request of someone by the name of Tiffany. Of course, I didn't have a clue who this Tiffany person was that Jeff was going on about, until he explained that she was the famous pop singer by the same name. And although the name sounded vaguely familiar, it took some brainwork to recall this bubble gum diva from years past. When Jeff mentioned the song "I Think Were Alone Now" that at last triggered whatever dim recollections I had related to the short-lived Tiffany phenomena, which hit its peak in the late 1980's. For those, like me, who've never been particularly enamored of top forty music, here's a little background on former teen queen, Tiffany.

Born Tiffany Renee Darwish, she began performing at an early age on the country and western circuit. In the early 80's, according to Jeff, Tiffany became an MK-ULTRA mind control victim at the diabolical hands of certain well-known country music stars that were later exposed in the controversial conspiracy tome, *Trance Formation In America* by Cathy O'Brien and Mark Phillips. Eventually, Tiffany was able to break free of her mind control programming and by the late 1980's became an MTV sensation. During this period, Tiffany's mother filed a missing person's report, and in return, Tiffany, then 17, filed for legal emancipation status as a minor. This made-for-TV production played itself out in a court trial in Los Angeles in 1988, with Tiffany eventually winning the case. This is where our story takes another bizarre twist...

As I later discovered, Jeff Turner--the unconventional hero of our story--appeared at the courthouse after the trial and presented Tiffany with a samurai sword and bouquet of flowers too congratulate her on the victory. When sheriffs saw the sword, they became predictably alarmed and placed Jeff under arrest, which in Jeff's estimation was a gross over reaction; he claimed it was an innocent mistake, a simple and loving gesture to show his support for Tiffany. Jeff later testified that he chose the sword and flowers because Tiffany likes Japan and receiving these items was considered a high honor in that country. Of course, when you see someone at a high profile trial brandishing a sword, it's the natural reaction of cops to act first and ask questions later. Charges were later dropped against Jeff when he repeatedly stressed to the authorities that the sword was dulled, and had been declared a ceremonial art object.

At a subsequent hearing, Jeff was charged with falsifying DMV documents to obtain Tiffany's home address and, as a result, was slapped with a restraining order. However, Jeff claims that the restraining order was not the actual doing of Tiffany, but that of her aunt, who had developed an irrational hatred of him. According to the Sept 27, 1989 edition of Santa Cruz Register-Pajaronian, Jeff was quoted as saying that Tiffany intended to marry him and, against her wishes, had been forced by family members to request the restraining order. Furthermore, Jeff claimed he was a distant relative to Tiffany, and that her mother and father had betrothed the two before their births per Lebanese tradition. In the aforementioned article, Turner stated that he was born to a "...Lebanese mother, who was part of this arranged marriage..." Turner further claimed that his mother's maiden name was Darwish, the same as Tiffany's, and he was unaware of his history until informed of it by Tiffany's family, who purportedly kept tabs on Jeff over the years.

At this point (in our trip down the rabbit hole) you might be thinking to yourself that Jeff Turner appears to be nothing more than an obsessed groupie or, at worst, a "stalker". But the more you look into the story, the less black and white it becomes. Actually, it's quite colorful. Even psychedelic...

The 1989 Register-Pajaronian article states that the petition for the restraining order alleged that "(Jeff) Turner wrote love letters to Tiffany. Turner said he wrote about 10 letters, but that Tiffany also wrote him love letters. Turner said she sent a cousin to stay in his rooming house and read the letters to him, in accordance, Turner said, with Middle Eastern tradition..." As it so happens, Douglas Hawes met this particular individual alleged to be Tiffany's cousin, whose name is Khalid Mansour. Mansour was living with Jeff in a boarding house in Santa Cruz Mountains in 1988, which is where Jeff claims he viewed the letters in question. Doug suspects that under heavy family pressures, and Tiffany's own gut instinct, she bailed out on the arranged marriage, as she didn't really know who Jeff was until she encountered him over a period of time, and had a chance to reassess the arranged marriage proposal. More on Jeff and Tiff later.

As previously noted, Tiffany was responsible for breaking up Tuesday Weld's purported occult organization and is currently attempting to dismantled K.M.'s satanic network, as well. In this regard, Tiffany is the leader of the "All Nations Movement", a super-secret society that is attempting to bring order to the world. Furthermore, Tiffany--whose Lebanese family has initiated her into the Sufi tradition--is now recognized as a master in international Sufi circles, and has used this influence to weed out negative elements that exist in certain secret societies and occult orders, such as those affiliated with K.M. and, formerly, Tuesday Weld.

Whatever the case, by the time we departed the Book Café my brain was suffering from severe sensory overload, saturated to the point where any further conspiratorial information was sure just to lap over my brainpan and form a lunatic puddle at my feet for me to ooze away in. Say "bye-bye"...

As Douglas Hawes readily admits, "You might be scratching your head about Jeff Turner, and I acknowledge he is an oddball, but he is indeed "inside the loop"... I have learned an immense amount of stuff through my association with him, over a 17 year period."

Afterwards, we returned to Jeff's apartment. As we made our way to his front door, we were discussing a couple different topics: 1) The

15

unkempt nature of Jeff's living quarters, and in particular his bathroom, and 2) A certain radionics/psychotronics device in Jeff's house that allowed him to quantum mechanically travel through time and space. (I just report this stuff, folks...) Anyway, I made the tongue-in-cheek quip that maybe Jeff could adjust the waves from his radionics machine and use it to psychotronically clean his bathroom, which got a chuckle out of both he and Doug. Of course, this might have been a mere courtesy chuckle on Jeff's part, humoring the wiseacre writer in his midst.

Once inside, we were barely able to navigate through Jeff's living room, scattered as it was with overflowing clothes piles amid bedding, books and magazines stacked to the ceiling. As we entered Jeff's bedroom--and I at last beheld his legendary psychotronic machine--I felt like I'd stumbled into a scene from Richard Linklater's *Slacker*. The machine itself consisted of a half dozen or so small transformer boxes with antennas poking out resembling items you could purchase at your local Radio Shack. Situated upon and around the antenna boxes were a potpourri of curiosities, which included a dozen or so small vials, one that said something like "Cosmic Energy Elixir"; assorted medallions that bore some seemingly mystical relation to "All Nations Movement" leader Tiffany Darwish; and several film developing envelopes with "Tiffany" scribbled on them. Next to this strange contraption--which I will henceforth refer to as the "Psychotronic Tiffany Shrine"--rested a chair with an old style looking football helmet on it that was hard-wired (you guessed it) into the Psychotronic Tiffany Shrine. Jeff apparently places this retro space age helmet on his head, then fires up the psychotronic whachamacallit, ostensibly beaming his cerebral cortex to Tiffany across time and infinite space. Or something like that. To tell you the truth, I didn't ask the whys and wherefores, for like I said, by this time my head was starting to pulsate in a feverish fashion, and there was a loud ringing in my nose.

Reverently, Jeff removed the photo envelopes marked "Tiffany" from his psychotronic shrine. Then, holding them up for us to see, thumbed through a half dozen or so photos that featured he and Tiffany posing happily together in a series of typical fan type shots taken at a Santa Cruz Boardwalk concert last summer, as well as the GlamourCon event in Los Angeles in November. Tiffany, now 32, interacts with Jeff at events such as these in a chummy fashion, which is surprising given their checkered history. According to Douglas Hawes, there's a lot that will be revealed about the Jeff Turner/Tiffany connection in the forthcoming documentary. In interviews from this film, Tiffany has apparently made some extremely revealing comments regarding her relationship with Jeff, particularly at the GlamourCon event where she displayed a surprising degree of nonchalance toward her former "stalker". In this regard, Jeff continues to make some interesting claims, such as the following in 2003 to journalist Wallace Baine of the Santa Cruz Sentinel: "(Tiffany) called me once at home. In the year 2000. October 7th. A Saturday."

From a chest of drawers, Jeff pulled out some photos of a display he'd put together a couple years earlier for the Santa Cruz Public Library. Presented under a glass case, it featured a photo of Tiffany arranged in the center of the display surrounded by an array books dedicated to time travel, alternate dimensions and the paranormal. Apparently, Jeff believes that Tiffany is not only the leader of a feel-good secret society and high Sufi master, but he also considers her a multi-dimensional time traveler. When I casually reached out to touch one of the Santa Cruz Library photos, Jeff moved it slightly out of my reach, so I pulled back my hand. I wasn't sure, at first, if he'd done so deliberately, or if it was just my imagination. A few minutes later, he showed us an 8x10 glossy of Tiffany, and when Doug attempted to touch it, Jeff nudge Doug's hand away with his elbow, so it immediately became apparent that he didn't like people touching his cherished Tiffany photos, for whatever reasons. Perhaps, he feels they're sanctified, and that if anyone touches them, it will drain the cosmic energy from the photos, or perhaps blasphemy the holy visage of "All Nations" leader Tiffany.

As late afternoon rolled around, I bid Jeff and Doug farewell, having a three-hour trek back home to the Sierras. Fortunately, I was able to get out of town just in time to beat the dreaded rush hour, which is no doubt the manifestation of much of the evil that Jeff perceives hovering over the greater Santa Cruz area like some dark, deadly angel.

Next time I see him, I'll have to ask if Tiffany can do something about the traffic.

A Trip To The Mound With Dock Ellis

When Pittsburgh Pirate pitcher Dock Ellis ingested a hit of LSD on June 12, 1970, little did he know that later that very evening he would accomplish one of the greatest feats in the history of professional sports. Around noon Dock dropped the acid in question, and was just starting to come on to it, when his girlfriend noticed in the newspaper that he was scheduled to pitch that night. Ooooopppps!

The game was in San Diego, a twi-night doubleheader, with a scheduled starting time of 6:05 p.m. Dock--who was in sunny LA--had his girlfriend drive him to LAX where he caught a 3:30 flight, arriving in San Diego at 4:30. An hour and half later, when Dock took his place upon the mound--in a situation he'd found himself numerous occasions--he felt like alien visitor to a somewhat familiar planet. He had just begun to peak, and an overwhelming sense of euphoria overtook him. Had the robotic function of throwing a ball not become habit to Dock over the years, he no doubt would have had a hard time functioning in this intense environment of athletic competition. But as he'd practiced these repetitive movements countless times before, Dock simply put his body on auto-pilot, focused his illuminated mind on its target--the catcher's glove--and let destiny take its cosmic course.

The ball--that historic day--was a blazing multicolored meteorite fired from Dock's nimble fingers with tremendous velocity, leaving a spiraling trail of shimmering shards in its passage. The catcher's mitt was a huge mellifluous magnet sucking the stitched orb telekinetically into its leather padding like a luminous egg returning repeatedly to the womb. The batters–with their bulbous, blubbery arms–wallowed futilely, swatting nothing more than the intoxicated air, as they waved with great force their Louisville Sluggers, leaving in their wake slow-motion rainbow-hued trails that hung momentarily in the heavy air before dissipating into gradual nothingness. The intense green grass rolled in hazy waves and the crowd was a multiple million eyed monster roaring maniacally, as the Pirate pitcher repetitively hurled the magical sphere across home plate, unhittable.

The sun burned that immortal day with brilliant intensity, or so it seemed to Dock, who flipped down his shades to not only dim its blinding rays, but to as well conceal his overly dilated pupils from any curious onlookers. Between innings–as he sat, blazing in the dugout– Dock closed his eyelids to discover naked dancing mermaids there washed ashore on steamy sands of satin and liquid lace. With shades over eyes he sat serenely silent by himself, swimming through an ocean of ONEness with the Universe, then landing on the sands to embrace the naked mermaids of his musing mind, and fondle their fins. His other teammates–aware that Dock was on his way to pitching a no-no– said nary a word to him, which was of course a baseball superstition/tradition; to leave alone a pitcher in the process of hurling a no-hitter, lest they jinx him into giving up a hit and losing the magic, which was just as well with Dock, 'cause he didn't feel like conversing to anyone anyhow; when he opened his eyes he was too busy watching the molecular fractal patterns fluctuate in the air.

Although one of the more accurate pitchers of his era, Dock's pitching control this monumental day–like his view of reality–was severely skewed. He unintentionally beaned two batters and walked a total of eight. But amazingly Dock remained unscathed, with not one run recorded against he and his powerful Pirates, though the bases were loaded (as was Dock!) several times during the course of the ball game. When all was said and done, Dock recorded a no-hitter. His first and last. Obviously this would've never happened had he not fucked up and dropped the acid unaware that a few hours later he would find himself on the mound before thousands, pitching in an altered state of mind.

This has been another memorable moment in stoned sports history.

When Camelot Grooved

We are all by now familiar with JFK's rampant womanizing and numerous sexual dalliances with secretaries and starlets behind White House walls while Jackie was off on spending sprees at Sacks Fifth Avenue. But one of the newest revelations to come to light in recent times was the alleged use of dangerous drugs during his one thousand days in office such as LSD, marijuana and cocaine, not to mention the bizarre meta-amphetamine mixtures brewed up by JFK's own personal physician, Dr. Max Jacobson.

Dr. Max, as he was affectionately known to his patients, came into prominence during the late 50's and early 60's, treating a veritable Who's Who list of celebrities with his bountiful bag of drugs from which he mixed together--like a mad scientist--feel-good potions, shooting them into the golden veins of the rich and famous, along with liberal doses of positive thinking psycho-babble.

Peter Lawford--a devoted patient of Dr. Max's--suggested to his brother-in-law, President Kennedy, that he invite Max to The White House so that Max could treat the Pres for the recurring back ailment he had suffered during WW2. (This was the very same injury that almost did JFK in when he had it operated on back in the 50's.)

In due time, Dr. Max became JFK's personal physician, running back and forth from New York to D.C. whenever the Pres' back started acting up, or when JFK was in need of a little pick me up. Occasionally, Dr. Max even traveled with the President. On JFK's European Tour, Dr. Max was there, lurking in the shadows with his mystical black bag of wonders, ready at a moment's notice to feed the President's veins via hypodermic needles filled with his magic potions.

Nobody ever really knew the exact contents of Dr. Max's injections, for the simple reason that they were always changing, due to whatever the doctor had on hand at the time. But the type of chemicals Dr. Max was most fond of, and which were ever present in his crazy concoctions, were the amphetamine/speed drugs, as well as such stimulants as B-vitamins, steroids, enzymes, placenta, bone marrow, animal organ cells and a whole host of other mood elevators to send his patients soaring out of his fashionable Manhattan offices like modern day Greek gods and goddesses on the wings of Icarus eventually in time to burn themselves out like so many wax-winged fools. His many rich and famous clients included the likes of Judy Garland, Truman Capote, Andy Williams, Mickey Mantle and Edward G. Robinson.

Truman Capote described the sensation of one of Dr. Max's shots as "instant euphoria. You feel like Superman. You're flying. Ideas come at the speed of light. You go 72 hours straight without so much as a coffee break. You don't need sleep, you don't need nourishment. If it's sex you're after, you go all night. Then you crash--it's like falling down a well, like parachuting without a parachute. You want to hold onto something and there's nothing out there but air. You're going running back to East 72nd Street. You're looking for the German mosquito, the insect with the magic pinprick. He stings you, and all at once you're soaring again."

Several books over the last few years--including *Acid Dreams* by Martin A. Lee and Bruce Shlain, *Flashbacks* by Timothy Leary, and *A Woman Named Jackie* by C. David Heymann--have all chronicled the escapades of an adventurous spirit by the name of Mary Pinchot, an artist and Washington socialite, whose husband was Cord Meyer, an agent of the CIA. Ms. Pinchot became acquainted with Timothy Leary during his Harvard days, requesting advice and samples of the good doctor's wares so that she could "turn on" those in "high places." Pinchot was convinced that if she could get certain prominent political leaders under the influence of acid, they would see that love is the answer to all the world's ills, then lay down their weapons, join hands with their former enemies and go off dancing into the daisies of harmonic conversion.

Mary Pinchot, as it turns out, was yet another of Johnny-we-hardly-knew-ye's conquests, having pierced her with the mighty sword of Came-a-lot on repeated occasions while under the influence of the drugs that Mary so graciously introduced him to. Allegedly, Jack and Mary on one stoned occasion smoked a couple joints, and when Mary started to spark a third, JFK was so bombed he told her he couldn't handle anymore, admitting to Pinchot that if he got anymore loaded he wouldn't be able to function effectively in the result of a National Emergency. Doomsday visions of his ol' buddy Nikita pushing the nuke button sending Ruskie bombers Washington's way arose in JFK's paranoiac marijuana muddled mind, and he wisely decided to let Mary loner the final doob in the interests of National Security.

Cocaine was also among the drugs allegedly used by Kennedy, as well as LSD. This is hinted at in *Flashbacks* and *Acid Dreams*, and I have no reason to doubt that on one occasion or another JFK did in fact blaze like a cosmic adventurer into the inner spaces of his mind, his psychedelic rocket ship fueled by Orange Sunshine™, landscaping New Frontiers.

Mary Pinchot-Meyer was riddled with bullets by unknown assailants and died just one short year after her boyfriend JFK had his own head blown off in Dealey Plaza.

A mind is a terrible thing to waste.

Rock N' Roll Minions of Satan

(co-written with Al Hidell)

In the late 1960's, Black Sabbath was one of the first rock groups to break through the countercultural banner waving in psychedelic Day-Glo colors of peace, love and drugs; ripping through the tattered fabric of the Summer of Love's idyllic symbolism, their dark fuzz tones and repetitive monster melodies paved the way for the occult-influenced rock of the 1970's and 80's. This sudden shift in perspective appeared to some to be the antithesis of everything the Summer of Love had stood for.

In Abbie Hoffman's autobiography, *Soon to Be a Major Motion Picture*, he describes a Black Sabbath concert he attended in the early 70's and the dark vibes that blasted from the amplifiers. Everything that had gone wrong at the end of the 60's, says Hoffman, was embodied in the negativity and fuzz tones booming from Geezer Butler and Tony Iommi's respective axes. Apparently the Rolling Stone's infamous 1969 Altamont concert—where the Devil metaphorically reared his malevolent horned head with the Hells Angel's stabbing murder of a spectator—had been a harbinger of things to come, just the tip of Satan's iceberg.

The Swingin' 6-6-60's

But did this dastardly influence begin prior to 1969 and before the first heavy metal devil bands burst on the scene, crooning their blasphemous ballads in homage to the Dark Prince? If you look into the psychedelic drug culture of the surrealistic 60's, you'll soon see the hooves of Lucifer hobbling about from the very beginnings of the Haight Street scene.

Anton LaVey, the high priest and founder of the San Francisco-based Church of Satan, became popular shortly before the psychedelic explosion. His church attracted a subculture of occultists as well as "beautiful people" who had tuned in, turned on, and dropped out, dedicating their lives to better living through chemistry.

One young beauty LaVey attracted was Sexy Sadie/Susan Atkins, who appeared in his "Witches' Sabbath" topless show playing the fitting role of a vampire. Three years later she would confess to licking blood from the knife that she used to kill actress Sharon Tate, when her theatrical vampire fantasy became reality during the Tate-LaBianca murder spree. Photos from this period show Atkins in her predestined role as vampire, wearing a long, open black robe revealing her nude body, as mock blood dripped from her lips. Later, of course, she fell into the loving arms of Father Manson, and the rest is dark history.

Charles Manson--who was deep into Satan as well as Christ, Hitler, Scientology, and the Beatles--showed up on the Haight shortly after his release from prison in the mid-60's. Manson immediately perceived the unlimited potential there: all the hopped-up impressionable minds waiting to be manipulated, including nubile teenage babes who would in good time and on his behalf commit grisly knife murders for their loving Messiah Chuck.

Bobby Beausoleil--who became one of Manson's most beloved hippie henchmen--was leader of a rock band named Orkustra around the time of Manson's arrival on the Haight and also starred in occultist Kenneth Anger's experimental film *Invocation of My Demon Brother* (1969). That film also featured Anton LaVey and a brief appearance by Rolling Stones' frontman Mick Jagger, who composed the soundtrack. Around that time Jagger also co-wrote the Stones' classic opus "Sympathy for the Devil."

Adam Gorightly

After working with Anger, Bobby Beausoleil sank to greater depths, burrowing into the deep dark pit of Helter Skelter accompanied by Sexy Sadie, Tex Watson, Patricia Krenwinkel, et al. Watson is perhaps the most guilty and dangerous of the Manson clan, including Manson himself. Watson has found Christ as his personal savoir and has a mail order ministry which he operates from prison, apparently making serious bucks and attracting true believers.

Satan's Top 40

Aleister Crowley—the renowned occultist and drug-sex experimenter—greatly influenced late 60's rock music as well as the contemporary heavy metal devil worshipers. Crowley died in 1947, but his evil spirit made a comeback in the 60's with the resurgence of interest in the occult. In fact, he appears among the myriad famous faces adorning the cover of the Beatle's *Sgt. Pepper's Lonely Hearts Club Band*. While that is certainly not indisputable evidence that the four Liverpudlian lads were also part of the Satanic underground, the Beatles were in fact one of the first rock groups to explore backward masking and the use of subliminal and "coded" messages in their songs. Hence, the "Paul is Dead" hoax and the Beatles song that Manson said inspired him, the title of which his followers wrote in blood on Sharon Tate's wall. (Hint: It wasn't "I Want to Hold Your Hand.")

In the early 1980's Christian broadcasters Paul and Jan Crouch produced one of the first television segments on backward masking. In this fascinating broadcast they played several rock songs backward, by artists including Led Zeppelin, ELO, and Black Oak Arkansas. On one tune from the *Black Oak Live* album could be heard the words: "Natas, Natas"—Satan spelled backward—raspily repeated over and over in a growl. Similarly, another researcher has demonstrated that Aerosmith's "Walk This Way" sounds a lot like "Hail Satan" when played backward. Some believe that such subliminal messages are poisoning the minds of susceptible listeners, who receive these sacrilegious missives surreptitiously and go on to perform evil deeds. Such an evil deed shook the small town of Northport, New York, in the summer of 1984. The incident involved three teenage boys, all from "good" homes: Ricky Kasso, Jimmy Troiano, and Gary Lauwers.

On the night of June 16 the three got together in a local park to do some mescaline, smoke some pot, and listen to a tape of Black

26

Sabbath's Ozzy Osbourne, who most assuredly "ruled". Within a few hours Lauwers was dead, stabbed at least thirty times in what police called a "sacrificial" and Satanic "cult killing." Kasso, it was said, had repeatedly ordered Lauwers to "say you love Satan" as he stabbed him, while Lauwers could only cry for his mother.

The police and the media labeled it a "Satanic" killing based on testimony given at the trial, as well as the presence near the scene of graffiti proclaiming such sentiments as "666" and "Satan Rules." Although there were clearly Satanic elements in the killing, as well as in the heavy metal music the boys often listened to, there is no evidence whatsoever that the music "compelled" the action or that the killing was part of organized "cult" activity. In fact, the killing appears to have had more to do with Kasso's drugged-out state and his anger at Lauwers for not having paid him for an order of mescaline. However, Kasso's jailhouse suicide, and the unexpected acquittal of Jimmy Troiano, raised the possibility that there was more to the story. (Another disturbing aspect of the killing was reported by David St. Clair in his book *Say You Love Satan*. He quotes a Northport real estate saleswoman's lament that "the worst thing" about the incident was that it "lowered property values.")

Heads Will Roll

In the 1970s *Creem* magazine was the rag to read if you wanted to keep abreast of what was going on in the heavy metal music scene. The hugely successful group Led Zeppelin was a frequent presence on its slick yet gaudy pages, with stories of Zeppelin guitarist Jimmy Page's famous haunted castle, once owned by none other than Mr. Aleister Crowley. Page is said to have reported various creepy apparitions, including a disembodied head rolling down the stairway. It seems Page was heavily involved in the supernatural, owning at one time an occult bookstore. Another item of interest concerning Page was that he composed music, not used, for *Lucifer Rising* (1970), a film by the aforementioned Kenneth Anger.

Rumor has it that the woes which befell Led Zep toward the end of the 70's were due to a curse upon the band caused by Jimmy Page's endeavors into the dark side. Given the premature death of Robert Plant's son, in addition to the drinking and drug-related demise of drummer John Bonham, some believe that the Zeppelinites were paying their just and due karma for years of reckless and deviant behavior—

specifically that of Jimmy Page, who was said to be a notorious drug abuser who spent his idle hours having sex with pubescent jailbait girls usually fourteen years of age or younger.

Standing at the Crossroads

Other performers besides Led Zeppelin may have been victims of Satanic curses, signing pacts that came due early in their music careers. Ironically, the guy who probably started it all was a man who inspired Jimmy Page: blues guitarist Robert Johnson. As legend has it, some time around the Great Depression, the struggling Johnson made a pact with the Devil while "standing at the crossroads." The deal provided him with awesome guitar-playing powers and a lasting influence on such rockers as Page and Eric Clapton. The catch was, as you might have predicted, an early death courtesy of a jealous husband.

Recently, guitarist Clapton experienced his share of tragedy when his toddler son apparently crawled out an open window and fell to his death. Also, Black Sabbath founder Ozzie Osbourne's fiery guitarist, Randy Rhodes—considered one of the greatest heavy metal players—died in a tragic plane crash at the height of success, while Ozzie and other band members watched from the ground.

And recall Jim Morrison, rock's premier delver into the darker side of human nature? According to Jerry Hopkins and Danny Sugarman's Morrison biography, *No One Here Gets Out Alive*, one night the Lizard King and a Scandinavian acquaintance named Ingrid Thompson snorted up a bunch of coke and shared a cup of ritual blood. They then fornicated, howling like banshees. After this wicked night of blood-drenched sex, Morrison woke up to discover the woman gone and himself and the sheets of his bed dry-caked with blood. This scared the shit out of wildman Jim, who rushed out of this den of wickedness only to die in Paris a few years later under mysterious circumstances.

A few months previously, Morrison had married witch Patricia Kennely—while at the same time betrothed to common-law wife Pamela—in a secret Wiccan ritual. However, it is important to note that witches (or Wiccans) like Kennely are not Satanists. Rather, they worship the ancient forces of nature: the Great Mother and her counterpart, the Horned God.

Then there's Jimi Hendrix. In an interview conducted after his death, one of his female friends stated that Hendrix had been prone to fits and seizures, where—driven to the point of madness—he'd pull his hair and go nuts, thinking himself possessed by evil entities. Was Hendrix himself the "Voodoo Chile"? Was Jimi tapped into strange spirits that in the end took his life at the pinnacle of a brilliant career?

The song has remained the same for many other rock legends, from Buddy Holly to Kurt Cobain. Even country crooner Hank Williams and rockabilly star Johnny Horton were said to have been married to a witch (the same woman) at the time of their deaths. After all the gifts of heaven and earth were bestowed upon them at young ages, they were taken away at the snap of a finger.

Satanic Underground

In *The Ultimate Evil*, author Maury Terry connects Charles Manson with various rock stars from the 60's who in turn were connected to a sinister Satanic underground of drugs, sex, ritual murder, and, ostensibly, the Process Church, a Satanic religious organization formed in England during the psychedelic 60's. Terry links this Satanic underground not only to the Tate/LaBianca murders, but also to the Son of Sam killings of the 1970's. Terry's thesis is that while David Berkowitz did in fact commit some of the Son of Sam murders, others were committed by this Satanic underground, namely an individual named Manson 2. (In 1993, Berkowitz himself claimed the involvement of unnamed others, part of what he called a Satanic cult, in the Son of Sam murders.)

According to Terry, Manson 2 played a pivotal part in the drug related murder of Roy Radin, producer of the film *The Cotton Club*. Actor Demond Wilson, of the 1970s sitcom *Sanford and Son*, appears to have also been connected with Radin and the cocaine fast lane, apparently working as a bodyguard for the producer. Soon after Radin's messy demise, Mr. Wilson found God and picked up a Bible, becoming a Baptist minister. Like Mansonoid Tex Watson and Demond Wilson, David "Son of Sam" Berkowitz is yet another Christian convert. Do ye see an odd pattern here or is it all just coincidence?

Two more rock stars alleged to have been connected to the celebrity Satanic underground were Mama Cass and John Phillips of the Mamas and Papas. After achieving phenomenal success with that group, John Phillips seemed to be the crown prince of the feel-good generation, a mover and shaker who knew all the right people and made all the right moves, financially and socially. Legendary were the parties at his posh pad in the Hollywood Hills, where a Who's Who of hip were known frequently to gather, getting high and cutting deals, plotting the new revolution of drugs, left-wing politics, and sexual liberation.

Author Maury Terry suggests that it was at some of these parties that the paths of Roman Polanski, Sharon Tate, and the rest of the star-struck Cielo Drive crowd initially crossed paths with the Manson clan. In a seemingly familiar pattern, misfortune soon fell upon Sharon Tate, Mama Cass, and John Phillips: Tate, of course, was brutally killed by the Mansonites; Cass soon died, done in by a heart condition; and John Phillip's life was nearly destroyed by his growing drug addiction. (Today Phillips is clean and drug-free, owing, in part, it is said, to the encouragement of friend Mick Jagger.)

Chuck Is Chic

Surprisingly, Manson had other celebrity connections. Prior to the Tate-LaBianca murders, Beach Boy Dennis Wilson is said to have been a Manson supporter. Manson and his "family" did in fact live in Dennis's house for a few months, supported by Wilson. Soon Manson was recording some songs at the home studio of Dennis's brother (and fellow Beach Boy), Brian Wilson. However, Dennis soon became frightened by Manson and fled the house, whose lease was almost up anyway. Manson and friends remained but were soon evicted by the landlord. Nevertheless, a song by Manson, with slightly altered lyrics, appears on the Beach Boy's album *20/20*. The original song was prophetically titled "Cease to Exist," but it is called "Never Learn Not To Love" on the album.

Because he dared to alter Manson's "sacred" lyrics, and also failed to get him a recording contract with producer Terry Melcher, Manson apparently grew to hate Dennis Wilson. Some believe that the Tate/LaBianca murders were actually a twisted warning to Terry Melcher, who was living at the murder scene just weeks before the killings occurred. In addition, a few days after the murders, Manson showed up at Dennis Wilson's house. Dennis was on tour, but Manson left a bullet and told the person answering the door to tell Wilson "this is for you."

Tragically, Dennis Wilson died an early and (according to the late conspiracy researcher Mae Brussell) mysterious drowning death in 1983. Was this the result of a Manson vendetta or curse? Did Dennis Wilson possess knowledge that would have turned Satan's mighty underground upside-down if revealed? Or did he die, as friends claim, in what was nothing more than a drunken swimming accident?

Before her own untimely death, Brussell was researching the military's involvement with the occult, Satanism and child abductions vis-à-vis Satanist and military intelligence officer Michael Aquino, among others. Did she discover certain secrets that led to her undoing? Some believe the cancer which killed Mae was created in a lab and injected, a scenario which Lee Harvey Oswald's killer, Jack Ruby, believed applied to his own fatal cancer. But that's another story...

In the 1990s singer Axl Rose has become Charles Manson's latest celebrity supporter. Rose has been criticized for recording a Manson song, wearing and selling Manson T-shirts at Guns n' Roses concerts, and sharing the profits with Charlie. Why is he doing this? Perhaps Rose is simply trying to attract publicity through his controversial actions. If so, he wouldn't be the first rock star to do so.

However, this might instead be a sign that a new generation of rockers has begun to play the same old dangerous game, courting forces more sinister than they or their fans can imagine.

Whatever Happened to "Psycho" Ronnie Rains?

ailed by its announcers as "America's fastest growing spectator sport!", Roller Games (and its rival league, Roller Derby) peaked in popularity during the early 1970's when it was in national television syndication. During this Golden Age, I'd religiously tune into the "Roller Game of the Week" on KTLA every Sunday night to hear that flamboyant trackside announcer Dick Lane, at least once a game, bellow: "Whoooooaaaaaaaaaa, Nelly!"

The Roller Game of the Week--hosted by this legendary team of the aforementioned Lane and his sidekick Bill "Hoppy" Haupt and his terminally bad hairpiece--each week featured the beloved Los Angeles Thunder Birds pitted against a rival bad guy team such as the Texas Outlaws, New York Bombers or Reilly's Western Renegades. What would normally transpire during the course of the Roller Game of the Week was an all out orgy of screaming, violence and overall bad behavior which usually culminated in a last second victory by the T-Birds, just when it appeared that all was lost!

As each Roller Game of the Week concluded, my brother and I—both of us by now worked into a lather by the spectacle we'd just witnessed—would wrestle our way to my bedroom, relentlessly punching each other as we made our passage. Then in our stocking feet--on the slick hardwood floor with a little table placed strategically in the middle of the room to approximate the center of the roller rink--my brother would whip me out on a jam and I'd slide swiftly across the bare, hardwood floor on imaginary roller skates, throwing elbows and delivering hip checks, crashing into the walls and alarming our parents as we skated around in our socks, beating the crap out of each other.

Such was our passion for Roller Games!

But as the early 80's rolled around, the wheels had come off the figurative skates of the Roller Games industry, due in part to the emergence of Vince McMahon's WWF, with the likes of such steroid-pumped superstar wrestlers as Hulk Hogan and the Macho Man, Randy Savage. Although a few feeble attempts to revive Roller Games have been attempted in recent years, its glory days most likely will never be recaptured. The last serious attempt was the short-lived RollerJam of a few years back, featuring juiced guys and shapely gals in sexy uniforms in a high-octane MTV generation version of Roller Games. But for all its flash and hype, RollerJam just couldn't capture the cheesy charm of its low budget predecessor.

Memories of the glory days of the banked track now bring a nostalgic lump to my throat as I think back to those roller stars of yore that soared around the track like comets in the night's sky, shining bright under the hot lights of the Olympic auditorium in Los Angeles. But of all those faded stars from the halcyon days of Roller Games, none burned brighter than the L.A. T-Bird's own "Psycho" Ronnie Rains, who was once described by an *L.A. Times* reporter as "a man who combines handsome physical features with the charm of Charles Manson."

Rains, a Los Angeles native, began competing as a flat track roller skater at age 11. As an amateur, Ronnie was 3-time national speed skating champion, along the way defeating some of the best skaters in the world, as he hitchhiked around the country competing in national championships. In his early twenties, Rains made the jump to the banked track, hired to his first Roller Games contract in 1963 with the New York Bombers. During the 60's, he spent several years with the Australian T-Birds, where he met his future wife, Australian skater Colleen Murrell. The best pure skater in the sport, Rains could skate backward on one skate better than most skaters could go forward on two, combining speed, agility and a manic personality, which captivated Roller Games fans around the globe.

In 1969, Ronnie returned to the New York Bombers as player/coach, assuming the classic role of the heel. On account of his over the top antics, opposing fans began taunting Ronnie with the nickname, "Psycho", which continually made him go berserk and cover his ears to drown out the deafening chorus of: "Psycho, Psycho, Psycho!" Conversely, Ronnie had the ability to work crowds into a frenzy, often inciting riots at other team's arenas.

Throughout his colorful career, Rains fluctuated between the roles of "good psycho" and "bad psycho", just as many of today's wrestling stars flip-flop between these good guy/bad guy personas as a marketing ploy. For many years, Rains--with his fondness for kicking opposing skaters in the face--was one of the reigning rogues of the game. Because of such bad guy tactics, Ronnie was the recipient of a bomb threat at his apartment in New York one time, and on another occasion was nearly shot by some irate fan that felt "The Psycho" needed to be put in his place. One time Ronnie enraged one spectator to the point that it caused the fellow to stand up without his crutches for the first time in years.

One of Ronnie's most infamous routines--circa 1972--centered around a German WW1 Kaiser helmet, the kind with a spike on top. Instead of the traditional helmet that jammers would normally use, "The Psycho" would wear this Kaiser helmet when he went out on a jam, the result of which made him seemingly invincible as he'd crash into opposing skaters and scatter them like bowling pins. For some reason, it never occurred to Ronnie to wear the helmet during the last jam of the game to score the winning points, thus his evil-hearted Bombers would always end up losing to those perennial good guy L.A. Thunderbirds. Eventually, Ronnie stopped wearing this magic helmet when it was officially banned by the Roller Games Commission on account of its evil mystical powers! That same year, Ronnie had a role in *Kansas City Bomber* starring Rachel Welch. Portraying the heel captain of a dastardly team called the Renegades, Ronnie's antics proved to be the most memorable and hilarious of all those Roller Games skaters appearing in the film.

Ronnie skated with the New York Bombers until 1973, when he switched sides and joined the L.A. T-Bird's, re-inventing himself in the image of the good natured psycho with a heart of gold. At the height of this "good guy psycho" phase Ronnie was much beloved in Los Angeles. In fact, it was the L.A. fans that turned around "The Psycho" nickname and started using it in a positive light, as over time Ronnie grew to appreciate the appellation.

A regular Harpo Marx on skates, Rains was a true comic genius. One minute he'd be racing around the track at 40 miles an hour, dodging in and out, throwing a shoulder here or an elbow there, knocking his opponents over the rail or into the infield. The next thing you'd know he'd be reaching down into the crowd and sweeping middle aged ladies off their feet, pulling them up to the railing and planting a big smooch on their cheeks.

Rains brought a creativity to the sport the likes of which hasn't been seen since. He had a thousand gags and gimmicks, like his famous "swivel hip" routine where he'd start doing this crazy little dance to juke opposing defenders, mesmerizing them just as a teammate, like little Ralphie Valladares, would come soaring around the corner on a jam and score! Other diversionary tactics including spinning in circles, making faces at his opponents, or biting them on the ankles.

Sometimes Ronnie would grab an opposing player and, much to their chagrin, start doing the jitterbug, high stepping and clowning, which would totally confound his roller-skated nemesis. Another stunt the Psycho mastered was to lay flat on his back and then scissors-kick an oncoming opponent, launching them over his head, where they would somersault in mid-air then land flat on their backs, grimacing in pain. On other occasions, Ronnie would suddenly grab the microphone from the track announcer and start eating the cord.

As Ronnie told *Roller Sport Illustrated* in 1974, "No one can ever predict what I am going to do next because I don't even know what it is. I'll be out there skating and suddenly an inspiration will hit me. A voice will descend to me from high above, far beyond the reaches of the arena, and like a lightning bolt it will instruct me with my next move.

"Just because I am the one chosen for these daring and essential deeds, the whole world is ganging up on me. Can you believe that as far away as Japan the people are up in arms against me and want to have me committed to an institution?"

———————

During his heyday, Ronnie transformed the banked track into his own personal canvas, painting these wacky landscapes. Occasionally you'd find him during a lull in action, sitting on the rails doing a pantomime of a motorcycle rider, complete with vocal sound effects, or an imitation of a channel swimmer or Superman. Other times he'd be sticking his tongue out at a referee.

Eventually, the other teams in the league become so alarmed at Ronnie's unpredictable behavior that they hired a man named Jess Adams to compile the infamous "Adam's Report" to determine Ronnie's sanity. Afterwards, when a reporter questioned the veracity of this report, implying that it was just another classic Roller Games ruse, Ronnie replied: "The Adams Report was on the up and up. It was all for real. The owners wanted me barred. They said I was psycho, when I was just eccentric."

In 1973, one of the Psycho's more memorable stunts took place at the Rose Bowl during a 4th of July fire works halftime display. For several weeks "The Roller Game of the Week" had been hyping how Psycho Ronnie was going to strap on a jet pack during the halftime show and fly out of the stadium. As promised, that's exactly what he did, (well, sort of) lifting off about twenty feet above the ground and spinning in circles, then returning back to earth. On that same night there was a tribute to that irrepressible trackside announcer, Dick Lane. During the fireworks show, a bust of Lane (laced with explosives) was ignited and burst into flames to the amazement of all those in attendance.

Each "Roller Game of the Week" featured a halftime interview where inevitably the star player on one team would challenge the other team's star to the obligatory "Match Race". Usually the interview culminated amid a flurry of fisticuffs and threats of career ending injuries, as the venerable Bill "Hoppy" Haupt would announce to the home viewing audience that a "5 laps anything goes match race!" between the two skaters would be held the following Saturday night at the Olympic Auditorium. Like clockwork, these halftime interviews would spark a mini riot in the crowd, as the camera panned the packed arena and Hoppy would yell out: "Better call Richmond 9-5171 right now before the tickets sell out!" Then--filled with anticipation of Psycho Ronnie going mano-e-mano with his nemesis to settle once and for all who was really the superior skater--I'd race to the phone and order tickets. Only later did I discover that these Sunday night telecasts were free admissions, which explained why the stands were always filled to capacity. This tried and true formula was the brainchild of legendary T-Bird owner Bill Griffith, Sr., who utilized such P.T. Barnum theatrics to promote his product. It was a formula that worked well for many years, but as the mid-70's rolled around, interest in Roller Games began to wane.

By the early 80's, the Roller Games league folded and Ronnie moved on. For a while he ran a gardening business in L.A., then later a flower shop, and soon faded from popular memory. Still, the legend of "The Psycho" burns bright with a few die-hard fans, who fondly remember when he reigned supreme over the banked track, flashing an infectious smile while pounding opposing skaters into submission. In fact, a small but fanatical following can be found these days on Internet messageboards and newsgroups, keeping the memory of Ronnie's skating days alive.

In fact, it was at one of these very Internet newsgroups that, much to my surprise and delight, I learned of Ronnie's current whereabouts. As it turns out, he is alive and well in Portland, Oregon, where he and his wife, Colleen, own and operate a Tommy's Burgers that is decorated with pictures and newspaper clippings from Ronnie's Roller Games career. On any given day you can find him there, reminiscing with customers about those heady days when he was known to the world as "The Psycho", the greatest Roller Games player to ever lace up a pair of skates.

For more about Ronnie "The Psycho" Rains visit: groups.yahoo.com/group/ronnieraines/

Postscript: The Tommy's Burgers Controversy

As we were going to press, I discovered a series of articles from 2003 chronicling some rather questionable business practices involving Ronnie Rains and the use of the "Tommy's Burgers" trademark, a famous Southern California restaurant chain.

According to "Miss Dish", food critic for the Willamette Week Online (www.wweek.com), "The signature (Tommy's) dish is a burger with a healthy dollop of a sweet meat-only chili, cheese, onions, pickle, tomato and mustard, and the chain artfully displays the blueprint of its masterpiece with a poster titled "Anatomy of an Original Tommy's Burger." "

When Miss Dish visited the Portland "Tommy's Burgers"--which formerly operated out of a building at Southwest 20th Avenue and Morrison Street, but switched to a cart after the restaurant closed---she discovered that it sported the same "Anatomy of an Original Tommy's Burger" image as its SoCal counterpart. When Dish asked one of the owners if they were connected to the California Tommy's, he replied: "We're from California...I knew Tommy." Afterwards, Miss Dish's research showed that this Portland version of "Tommy's" had no affiliation to the "Original Tommy's" of Southern California.

After this article appeared, the Portland "Tommy's" received letters from the Original Tommy's lawyers. Subsequently, the name was changed to "Ronnie's", and then shortly after to "Salt & Pepper".

Moral of the story: You can't keep a good psycho down!

John Lilly, Ketamine and The Entities From ECCO

In the early 70's, John Lilly was introduced to the drug Ketamine by Dr. Craig Enright in the hopes of alleviating the pain associated with Lilly's chronic migraine headaches, which he had been suffering like clockwork--every 18 hours--for most of his often-adventurous life.

Lilly, at the time, was at Esalen Institute conducting seminars when one of these massive migraines hit him. In situations such as these, Lilly withdrew into privacy, to suffer alone through the many endless hours of severe discomfort. It was at this time that Enright suggested to Lilly that he enter into the Esalen isolation tank and receive an injection of Ketamine, in the prospect that it would help cure him of his affliction. Lilly in the past had tried a similar experiment with LSD, but it proved unsuccessful, and the terrible headaches persisted. In the earlier LSD-assisted experiment, Lilly attempted to reprogram his human bio-computer in such a way as to eliminate the faulty circuits that were causing him such distress. The experiment failed, but now once again Lilly the Scientist was searching for a cure to his malady.

As Lilly floated in the isolation tank fluid, Enright injected him with 35 milligrams of Ketamine (K). Within a few minutes, Lilly could actually visualize the migraine pain moving out through his skull, to a point three feet away from his position in the fluid. As the pain levitated there in apperceived space, Lilly felt no pain whatsoever for some twenty minutes, until it once again reentered his head. When Lilly began moaning and groaning, Enright injected him with another 70 milligrams. This time Lilly felt the pain moving farther away, twelve feet this time. Thirty minutes later the migraine lightning bolt of pain came rushing back, lodging itself once again into Dr. Lilly's head. Enright reloaded his syringe and shot the good doctor up with 150 milligrams. This time when the pain vacated Lilly's head it kept on going and didn't come back; clear over the horizon, never to be seen again. An hour later, after the K wore off, Lilly climbed out of the tank, a new man.

A month later, when the regularly occurring migraine did not return, Lilly was amazed. During his psychedelic research of the early

'60s, Lilly was one of the early pioneers in charting the inner landscapes of the human brain with LSD inside his self-developed isolation tank. Within those dark, still waters of the soul, Lilly ingested heavy doses of acid and delved deep into his mind to imprint and re-program his mental circuits toward enlightenment and self-realization. But where LSD had failed in defeating the migraine problem, Ketamine had now apparently succeeded.

A week later when Doctor's Enright and Lilly met at the Esalen isolation tank, they agreed to join forces and conduct a joint research into the effects of Ketamine as a possible programming agent. The movie *Altered States* was based on one of their initial experiments. On that memorable occasion, Enright injected himself with a measured dose of K and--with Lilly observing--began a strange odyssey into the primal/archetype regions of his psyche. Unbeknownst to Dr. Lilly, Enright had reprogrammed himself "to return to the prehominid origins of man." Enright, in this programmed "altered state", displayed all the typical features, movements and sounds of an Ape Man; hopping around in a crouching position, grunting, growling, ranting and howling, gesticulating and frantically shaking his arms. While all of this high weirdness was going on, Lilly assumed that Enright was having some sort of seizure. Though in close proximity with each other throughout the entire experience, the separate realities they were experiencing were of entirely different natures. Enright's reality consisted of a confrontation with a leopard, which he drove away with all his arm flailing, grunting and wild gesticulations. Finally, Enright climbed up into a tree (that Lilly couldn't see) and stared down at his friend and colleague from the branches above.

From this experiment, Enright and Lilly drew three important conclusions: "First, one's internal reality could differ radically from the external reality in which one was participating, even with regard to prominent features of the physical environment. Second, the person might remain active physically in the external environment, in a manner not responding closely to one's internal experience of this activity. And third, one could remain totally oblivious to this disparity." Given these conditions, Lilly and Enright agreed that it would be a good idea at all times to have a "safety man" monitoring the experiments; to observe the proceedings and insure that those under K's influence could do no physical harm to themselves and others. With both men being trained physicians the obvious choice to fill these roles were themselves, alternately switching positions as "safety man" and "explorer."

One determining factor in Lilly's decision to continue experimenting with K was its measurability. Unlike other programming agents he had used in the past, K's effects were extremely predictable, in that you could determine exacting levels of dosage to correspond with the desired effect one wished to experience. Whereas other mind expansion agents such as LSD and psilocybin are often more unpredictable in regards to the facilitation of desired preprogramming. This brings to mind a possible correlation between Ketamine and DMT, where each of these drugs--administered at certain exacting dosages--apparently summon forth extraterrestrial or other-dimensional entities. High doses of psilocybin have affected this response in some users--Terrance McKenna, among others--who have communicated telepathically with alien intelligences under the mushroom's otherworldly aegis. But psilocybin's effects are quirky. Perhaps this is why the measurability--and predictability--of K so appealed to Dr. Lilly. In this manner the scientific method could presumably be followed to achieve the desired results.

In later experiments, Lilly failed to heed his own advice, becoming so enraptured in his Ketamine exploration that he would forego the earlier agreed upon "safety man" and started working "without a net." This led to an almost fatal consequence when one day, under the influence of K, Lilly climbed into his hot tub. When he realized the temperature was too hot, Lilly futilely attempted to climb out, but in so doing his muscles lost their strength and he collapsed. Lilly was conscious at this point, but due to the effects of K, he was unaware of the external reality that he was drowning. He was conscious only of his internal world. As fate would have it, a friend of Lilly's, Phil Halecki--who found himself driven by a sudden sense of urgency--decided at this time to phone Dr. Lilly. Lilly's wife Toni fielded the phone call and, at Halecki's insistence, went to summon John, only to find him lying face down in the water, breathless and blue. Fortunately, Toni was able to revive her husband using mouth-to-mouth resuscitation, a technique she had learned only a few days earlier from an article in *The National Enquirer*.

Nonetheless, this close brush with the grim reaper's scythe didn't deter Lilly from further solo flights on K. It only reaffirmed his deeply held conviction that his life was being watched over by higher powers of an extraterrestrial origin. Lilly referred to this network of sublime entities as ECCO, an acronym for "Earth Coincidence Control Office". Lilly was positive that all of these coincidences in his life (such as Halecki's life-saving phone call) had been arranged by higher forces, and that whatever misfortune fell into his path along the road to knowledge, ECCO would be there to guide him safely through the dark tunnel to the light.

But ECCO was there not only to guide Lilly through his mind-bending research. These extraterrestrial benefactors were also there to test Lilly, to help him overcome his deepest, darkest fears with psychic-shock therapy. One evening after an injection of K, Lilly sat watching TV when an alien representative of ECCO appeared and--with some advanced form of psychic surgery--bloodlessly removed John's penis, nonchalantly handing it over to him. "They've cut off my penis," Dr. Lilly exclaimed. His wife Toni came to the rescue and pointed out to John that his penis was still intact. Upon closer examination of his member, Lilly saw that the ET's had replaced his normal human penis with a mechanical version that could become voluntary erect when he wanted it to. An hour later, after the effects of the K wore off, John Lilly found his normal human penis in place of the mechanical one, exactly where it had always been.

Later on, as the frequency of his use of K increased, Dr. Lilly began having contact with another alien intelligence agency, which he called SSI, short for Solid State Intelligence. SSI was a supercomputer-like entity, much in the same techno-mystical vein as Philip K. Dick's VALIS. But unlike VALIS, SSI was of a malevolent nature, at odds with ECCO. SSI's apparent goal was to conquer and dominate all biological life forms on Earth. To combat SSI, ECCO enlisted Lilly in this archetypal battle of good against evil, charging him with the mission of alerting the world to these solid state beings of evil intent.

To further confirm the dual existences of these two opposing alien intelligence networks, Lilly was given a sign, and message, in the autumn of 1974. Flying into Los Angeles International Airport (LAX), Dr. Lilly saw the comet Kahoutek out of the southern sky. Momentarily the comet grew brighter. At this point a message was laser-beamed into Lilly's mind, which said: "We are Solid State Intelligence and we are going to demonstrate our power by shutting down all solid state equipment to LAX."

Dr. Lilly shared his foreboding message with his wife Toni, who was seated next to him. A few minutes later, the pilot instructed the passengers that they were being diverted to Burbank due to a plane that had crash-landed near the runway and had knocked down power lines, causing a power failure at the airport.

As his haphazard use of K intensified, so did the warnings of imminent dangers regarding the survival of mankind, provided by ECCO via 3D Technicolor images beamed into Lilly's mind. These visions were of an apocalyptic nature; scenes of nuclear annihilation seen from an alien's eye view in outer space. The world powers needed to be alerted of this impending tragedy immediately to enable them to avert widespread global devastation, ECCO instructed, or it would be too late. I find it interesting that ECCO's message to Dr. Lilly was much the same as those delivered to the early saucer contactees: our planet was on a collision course toward destruction; all atomic weapons must be dismantled if our planet was ever going to have a chance of surviving in the future. The only difference was that the enemy was us, not "them." Nevertheless, rampant technological progress was to blame for the sorry state of the planet, regardless if it was being facilitated by alien intelligences, or humans.

After three weeks of hourly K injections, Lilly decided that he would travel to the east coast to warn political leaders and members of the media of the threat posed by SSI. In New York, he phoned the White House to warn then President Gerald Ford about "a danger to the human race involving atomic energy and computers." A White House aide fielded the call and, although quite aware of Dr. Lilly's impressive credentials, was not convinced of the urgency of the matter, and informed him that the President was unavailable.

A young intern, who had been assigned to Lilly during this time, figured the good doctor had finally flipped his high intelligent lid and attempted to have him committed to a psychiatric hospital. Once again ECCO intervened. Lilly had friends in many high places, one of which was the director of this hospital, who saw to it that his old friend was released in short order. When the intrepid intern attempted to commit Lilly to another psychiatric hospital, the same scenario unfolded, and Lilly was once again released. The young intern could only shake his frustrated head in disbelief.

———

Still following the lead of ECCO, Dr. Lilly continued his ever-escalating injections of K in order to remain in contact with the "space brothers." Soon, though, his sources started to dry up due to concerns by his colleagues that Lilly had gone off the deep end. Consequently this led Lilly in search of other long acting chemicals that would provide him with the same effects as K, but for a greater duration. During the experimental trial of another drug of similar nature to K, Dr. Lilly received a phone call from his wife Toni requesting that he bring her spare set of car keys, because she had locked her set in her car. Since she was simply down the road a bit, Lilly jumped on his ten-speed and proceeded to peddle down the road to make the delivery.

John Lilly, Ketamine, and The Entities from ECCO

When Dr. Lilly decided to ride his ten-speed bike down the road to meet his wife, the drug had not yet taken full effect. But midway through his trip, Lilly was zapped by its intoxicating magic and instantly felt quite wonderful with the wind blowing deliciously through his hair; it was as if he'd taken a trip down memory lane to the days of his free wheeling youth. Unfortunately, this flashbackful sense of euphoria came screeching to a disastrous halt when the bike chain suddenly jammed, and he was catapulted onto the harsh reality of the concrete pavement, puncturing a lung, breaking several ribs, and suffering cranial contusions. This bicycle crash resulted in several days of hospitalization, where Dr. Lilly was once again visited by the otherworldly representatives from ECCO, who told him he had a choice: He could go away with them "for good" or remain on the planet, mend his body and concentrate on more worldly affairs. The good doctor wisely chose the latter. With this decision came a turning point in his life, and a conscious effort to focus his remaining years not only on more earthly matters--as opposed to the whims and wishes of ECCO--but to dedicate the rest of his life to his wife, Toni, and their soul mate journey together through physical time and space.

Many paranormal parallels can be drawn from the experience of John Lilly, one such being the so-called Near Death Experience (NDE), where Guides, as he called them (the two representatives from ECCO) appeared to Lilly much as figurative angels bathed in light do to others who have experienced NDE. Often, as the seemingly near dead hover before this subjective light, they are offered a choice much similar to the one given Dr. Lilly by his otherworldly benefactors from Earth Coincidence Control Center: *Should I stay or should I go?*

Not long after this second brush with death, Dr. Lilly's close friend and Ketamine research partner, Craig Enright, was involved in a head on collision in the fog on coast Highway One in California. As Enright lay upon his death bed, he was visited by Dr. Lilly, who took Enright's hand in his, and made the following statement: "It's not so bad to die, Craig. I've been to the brink myself a few times, and I've seen over the edge. The Beings have told me on several occasions that I was free to go with them, but I decided to stay here and continue my work in this vehicle that everyone calls John Lilly; they showed me that I am one of them. 'You are one of us'. I know that you know this because we've been there together. Whatever you do, Craig, I love you." On the very next morning, Dr. Craig Enright shed his mortal coil.

Thus ended another chapter in Dr. Lilly's often adventurous life.

Somewhere Over The Rainbow, Man

Rockin Rollen Stewart was a familiar presence to sport's fans. Even though you have probably never heard his name before, you'll remember the banners he used to display at sporting events, reading 'John 3:16'.

After garnering his first frenetic fifteen seconds of Warholian fame at a Portland Trailblazer Basketball game in 1977, Stewart sought to spread his message further and further afield. For years he was seen making a spectacle of himself at various sporting events in a huge rainbow colored wig, smiling from ear to ear with wide eyes, hoisting high in his busy hands giant placards with biblical passages writ upon them, as he gleefully bounced around, clad in fake fur loincloths.

Rollen, through years of practice (and spending every last cent he had to attend these sporting events) developed an innate talent for strategically positioning himself--much to the constant chagrin of network cameramen--in such a way as to steal the limelight from the televised proceedings while spreading The Word of the Lord.

"He's a pest, " an NBC executive once snorted. "We try to take him out of a shot whenever we can."

"He got to be a terrific distraction," seconded ABC sports producer Chet Forte. "He would station himself behind home plate and our camera would view over the pitcher's shoulder and it was very annoying seeing this guy waving the signs and all."

Occasionally, those annoyed by Stewart's actions would provoke security guards. "You know you're not wanted when they send security guards to walk you out of your seat," Stewart once said. Stewart claimed he was hounded by authorities at the 1984 Olympics in Sarajevo who took him for a spy, thinking his JOHN 3:16 placard was some sort of coded message.

Stewart became known as "The Rainbow Man" due to the aforementioned rainbow-hued wig of which he adorned his anointed, holy-madman-head, buzzing as it did with the divine resonance of The Lord. It was sometime during the late 70's when I first spotted Stewart on my home TV screen at a sporting event (this was before he was born-again and rescued by Jesus from a dark abyss of sexual promiscuity and wanton drug abuse. Stewart later said of that period of his life: "I said I was going to sail around the world on my water bed.")

At the height of his popularity, Stewart appeared in a commercial for Anheuser-Busch, and was paid to attend parties looking his outlandish self, rainbow hair, loin-cloth and all. His character was featured on *Saturday Night Live, St. Elsewhere* and *The Tonight Show.* Cartoonist Charles M. Shultz drew The Rainbow Man into his cartoon *Peanuts* standing alongside good ol' Charlie Brown.

But, unfortunately, toward the end of the 80's, things started to unravel for The Rainbow Man. In a 1982 interview with *Golf Digest* magazine, Stewart was quoted as saying: "I was living on my ranch...and my life revolved around sex and drugs. I wasn't happy, though, and one night I had a religious experience and was born again as a Christian."

This historic conversion took place after the 1980 Super Bowl in Pasadena. As Stewart recalled, "I had gone in my fur loincloth and wig. The girls loved it. Everywhere I walked, they were patting my butt. I could have held a thousand women in my arms that day, and yet I walked out of there sad. It was the shallowness. I was being seen all over the world, but never as myself." That night, after returning to his hotel room he found Jesus, while watching a television show called *Today In Bible Prophecy.* "I fell to my knees there in that room and allowed Jesus to take control of my life."

Subsisting on one meal a day, and smoking massive quantities of pot, Stewart began a blitzkrieg for the Lord, working 12 sporting events a month as he fervently flashed his JOHN 3:16 message on placards, signs and T-Shirts, spreading The Lord's Word in his own unique fashion. (The message of the Gospel according to St. John, chapter 3, verse 16, is, "For God so loved the world, that He gave his only begotten Son, that whosoever believeth in Him should not perish, but have everlasting life.")

In 1984, he met Margaret Hockridge, a born-again grade school teacher, at a church in Virginia. Margaret found herself, "in awe of him." Smitten, the two bought a Toyota van and hit the road for the Lord. Ten months later the couple were married in St. Louis. The bride dressed in mauve, and Stewart wore a T-shirt emblazoned with the message 'Jesus is Coming.'

As the 80's progressed, Stewart fell deeper and deeper into his strange vocation, driving more than 50,000 miles a year, and traveling to more than 100 sporting events. The strange thing is, Stewart didn't even like sports. In fact, as he told *People* magazine in 1988: "I despise sports. People who go to sporting events are like the Romans who went to watch the lions eat the Christians. I know I'm a strange and unusual vessel. But we're sincere about this."

He didn't much like TV either. "I realize now television is a tool of Satan," he said. "I never watch TV unless it's to figure out my own strategy so that I can appear on it." This he did to perfection, figuring out where cameras were located and calculating how tight the camera angles were. Then he could place himself in a position so when the camera came on him Stewart was ready to bounce about and spread his tutti-frutti word o' the Lord.

Stewart was a stickler for details, especially when it came to his advertisements for God. According to Hockridge, his now ex-wife, he blew up at the 1986 World Series at Shea Stadium. Stewart figuratively flipped his wig and tried to choke Hockridge when she stood in the wrong spot with her JOHN 3:16 placard, incurring the righteous wrath of the rainbow-headed one. His mood, Margaret said later in a *People* magazine interview, was "constantly up and down." By 1990, Margaret had had enough, and filed for divorce.

After the breakup Stewart apparently became more unstable. In May 1991 an arrest warrant was issued, accusing him of 4 stink bomb attacks in Orange County, California. The warrant charged Stewart with setting off foul-smelling bombs at the Crystal Cathedral in Garden Grove; a Christian bookstore in Garden Grove; at the Trinity Broadcasting Studio in Tustin; and at the offices of the *Orange County Register* newspaper in Santa Ana. According to the authorities, Stewart assembled the stink bombs using a timing device, a knife and an acid filled balloon.

At the 1991 Masters golf tournament, the authorities detained Stewart after he allegedly set off a remote controlled air horn, a loud buzzer and several colorful smoke bombs just as Jack Nicklaus was preparing to putt on the 16th green. Stewart was released after tournament officials declined to press charges.

"The same type of device went off at the Foreman-Holyfield fight," Santa Ana Police investigator Ferris Buckles said. "But investigators there kicked it down a sewer storm drain and we don't have the evidence."

A year before, Stewart had been arrested for disturbing the public at The American Music Awards in Los Angeles after he tried to toss skunk sacs into the audience. Stewart said he wanted to show the public that "God thinks this stinks."

Matters came to a head in late September 1992, when Stewart was arrested after holding a maid hostage in the Hyatt Hotel next to Los Angeles International Airport. Stewart, reported the *Los Angeles Times*, held the police at bay with threats that he had a bomb. When the stand-off continued well into the evening, police officers used what they called 'flash-bang' grenades to stun a wigless Rainbow Man and storm the seventh-floor room where he was under siege. A 38-year-old housekeeper was found uninjured after having locked herself in the bathroom. The police apparently decided to make their move after Stewart threatened to fire a pistol at planes landing at the airport. A few hours after the incident, as the police were driving Stewart away, reporters asked him why he had done it. "To get the word out ," he shouted back, flashing a smile.

The incident began at 9:15 on the morning of September 22nd, when Stewart walked into a vacant room at the Hyatt, taking the cleaning lady, Paula Madera, by surprise. Madera immediately ran into the bathroom and locked herself in, figuring rightly that Stewart was some kind of crazy. It was at this point the Rainbow Man decided to light two small fires, which attracted attention to himself.

In short order, LA Police Department ordered up the SWAT Team, bomb squad and several fire engines to deal with the situation. While all this commotion was going on outside, Stewart was posting biblical placards in his hotel room window so they could be read from the ground below. One was an apocalyptic verse from the New Testament referring to the passage: "The heavens shall pass away with a great noise, and the elements shall melt with fervent heat."

At 5:45 PM--when Stewart threatened to harm his hostage and start taking pot shots at jetliners as they passed near the hotel--the police decided to act. Shortly after, the SWAT team stormed the room, using flash-bang grenades to disorient Stewart. At the scene police found Stewart's infamous blue, red, yellow, green, purple and pink Afro wig, along with a high caliber pistol, various incendiary devices, three day's worth of food, as well as Bibles, religious tracts and poetry.

According to another LA Times article, Stewart's motive for taking a hostage was so he could alert the world that Armageddon was nigh at hand.

"He thinks the second coming of Christ is on the way, and he wants to spread the word," said LA Police Detective Tom King. "I don't consider him to be a nut. I consider him to be a religious zealot."

Charles R. Taylor, the baptist minister whose TV show *Today in Bible Prophecy* inspired Rollen's religious conversion, echoed Officer King's sentiments. "He's not dangerous, he won't hurt anyone." Taylor, who went to the hotel during the hostage drama in an unsuccessful attempt to persuade Rollen to surrender, described him as "a little on the fantical side. He meant well, but he took the wrong approach."

Others, though, felt Stewart posed a genuine threat. "This is not Bozo the Clown," said LA District Attorney David P. Conn. "He is a sick and dangerous man."

Talking to *People* magazine, Stewart seemed unworried that some considered him dangerous. "I was asked by the psychiatrists here if I hear voices," said Rollen during an interview conducted in prison. "I answered, 'No, I'm not hearing voices. But I've been hearing the voice of God for years."

On July 13th, 1993, "Rockin'" Rollen Stewart was sentenced to three terms of life imprisonment for his role in the hostage drama. This might seem extreme when one takes into account that Rollen Stewart never hurt a flea, but many felt he had the capacity to go further. LA's deputy district attorney Sally Lipscomb described him as "a David Koresh waiting to happen. He has the same beliefs and he stands by them so strongly he's willing to die or kill for them."

During sentencing in the LA Superior courtroom, pandemonium erupted, as Stewart began a rambling end o' the world rant, conducted at top volume. Upon being wrestled to the floor by deputies, he shouted: "Forgive them, Lord, for they know not what they're doing!" While that was going on, the maid who had been trapped in the hotel room by Rockin' Rollen, wept in the rear of the courtroom.

In February 1994 Stewart was sentenced to an additional five years for his Orange County stink bomb escapades.

"This man would not let any crime get in the way of getting his message out," said deputy district Attorney M. Marc Kelly. "We felt he deserved to be punished and the public of Orange County deserved to have him put away for as long as possible." Municipal Court Judge Elva Soper described Rollen as a "danger to the community."

That this danger might have been real was brought to light by the *Los Angeles Times*, which reported in September 1992 that Stewart had contemplated killing President George Bush and took steps toward assassinating then Presidential candidate Bill Clinton. According to District Attorney David Conn, Stewart bought a .45 caliber handgun at the time of Clinton's campaign visit to LA, then went to the Boneventure, where Clinton was staying, to shoot him. He aborted his plan when he became aware of the heavy security surrounding Clinton. At around the same time he was also spotted at a speech given by the Arkansas governor.

Stewart's word spread, despite his position on the fringes of society. Though many saw Stewart as a lone-nut evangelist, he was actually part of a small and close knit group of "televangelists" whose "television ministries" were funded by a vast network of Christians sympathetic to their message of the imminent second coming of Christ. This network enabled Stewart to generate the money necessary to finance his activities, and to send his helpers to sporting events. One of Stewart's evangelical allies, Doug Hill, told the *Arizona Republic* in January 1992, "To the best of my knowledge, there are only seven of us. With as many games as we're on, most people think it's a hundred people."

Doug Hill first saw the master of the medium--the ubiquitous Rollen Stewart--at a football game in the mid-80's, and thought to himself, "Wow, I could do that, too!" So Hill made himself up a John 3:16 placard, bought a rainbow-fro, and then followed faithfully the footsteps of his inspiration across the TV screens of America, waving his religious signs much to the dismay of TV sport producers.

Whether the number of copycat followers of Stewart was actually two, seven, or a hundred, it gives one cause to ponder the effect of charismatic characters such as "The Rainbow Man", and their ability to attract followers together in a common cause, fueled by an intense belief that Armageddon is on the horizon, and that drastic action must be taken to spread word of The End Times.

In the final analysis, I believe Rollen Stewart became disillusioned with not only his fleeting fame in the late 80s, as more and more TV directors became wise to his ploys and were able to limit his on-screen antics; but also with the growing realization that his message was not being taken seriously. Perhaps this is why he decided to up the ante and secure his rightful place in martyrdom with the likes Jim Jones and Dave Koresh, albeit on a smaller, less bloodier scale, than his two charismatic counterparts.

Jim Keith, Burning Man and "Wounded Knee"

During his days editing *Dharma Combat*, Jim Keith gave voice to a number of dissident writers, who--without his assistance-- would have sunk ever deeper into literary obscurity. Among these was Jeff Lewis, one of the most unique and controversial voices to emerge from the alternative 'zine scene of the late 80's/early 90's.

In Jeff's case, "sunk" seems an apropos term, as his writings plumb the depths of the dark subconscious, and it is through sinking into these turgid waters--and his search for "sunken" treasures--that Mr. Lewis attempts an ascent above those ancient forces which, throughout human history, have held men as slaves, in waking reality and in the realm of dreams. In these respects, Lewis is a poet engaged in spiritual warfare.

"'Much of my work,'" says Lewis, "is based upon personal experience in dreams, and describes the long process of recovering personal control in the realm of the unconscious. The recovery of active metaphysical vision and will with which to work in the depths of the unconscious is, I believe, the primary task of the poet, creative person-- and the means by which we may regain, not only the singing ability of the mythical Orpheus, but also his power."

As I interpret Jeff's dream-work, it more than just affects his immediate surroundings, but extends outwards, intuitively grasping the emotional or psychic turmoil of others, and--like a shaman gazing deep into the ethers for answers--he has taken it upon himself to work out the chaos of the world. *Order from Chaos*. But before we get too deeply into Jeff Lewis' "wounded knee" revelations, let's recount Jim Keith's final days.

Most readers of *SteamShovel Press* should be familiar with the late Mr. Keith--noted conspiracy author and researcher--who met his untimely death via a circuitous route which led through *Burning Man*, an "alternative culture" festival that takes place each year in the Black Rock Desert near Reno, Nevada. Your humble reporter has twice attended *Burning Man*--in '97 and '98--and to put into words what takes place there could hardly be captured in the short span of this article. Call it performance art meets fireworks/pyrotechnics nudity techno-tribalism pagan ritualism SubGenius Devivalism topped by a

50

liberal sprinkling of booze and psychedelics--and that's just what happens on the first day! To get a general overall feel of the event, do a web search for *Burning Man*, and you'll turn up all kinds of interesting links and high weirdness.

As the story goes, Keith broke his knee falling from a three-foot stage at *Burning Man*, and the next morning went to Washoe County Medical Center to get it examined. Hospital reports state that related kidney problems developed soon after, preventing immediate surgery. Three days later--on September 7th--when surgery was finally performed, Keith died due to a fatal blood clot that was released from his leg, and traveled into his lung.

Rumors soon began circulating through the conspiracy research community about the true nature of Keith's untimely passing. Many have pointed to his last article for the now defunct webzine *Nitro News,* the results of which presumably sealed Jim's fate due to his naming the physician who declared Princess Diana pregnant at the time of her death. One should also bear in mind the list of those who've died mysterious deaths in relation to the Clinton Presidency, one of whom was researcher Danny Casolaro. The only published work yet to delve to any great extent into the Casolaro affair is *The Octopus* by Jim Keith and *Steamshovel Press'* editor Kenn Thomas. From this jumping off point it could be conjectured that Jim Keith is but another in a long line of those who've gained infamous mortality vis-à-vis Clinton's ever-growing Death List. For anyone unfamiliar with this list, there are no doubt many sources available on the Internet where it can be accessed, and one quick perusal of said will tell you that any one associated with Clinton in the early years of his candidacy-cum-presidency possessed some terribly bad luck. With this being said, it could have been any one of a number of conspiracies that attributed to Keith's death.

But perhaps there's an even more obscure explanation for Jim's premature passing, which brings us back full circle to Jeff Lewis' dream-work. Prior to receiving news of Keith's death, Jeff had a perplexing dream, as he termed it to me; a dream in which terrible wounds appeared on his knees, apparently fatal in nature. The inference here is that Jeff had psychically transferred the trauma of Jim Keith's ordeal--in essence, assuming Keith's ordeal--so that in some manner he could work it out, and heal these "knee wounds", in the same way a shaman accepts the pain of others, assuming sickness in order to dispense with it, to transmute it into a transcendent form. I would only add here that Lewis--although he does, in my opinion, take on a sort of shamanistic role in his dream-work--has never referred to himself as such. As a shaman is one who's immediately identified with channeling "gods", this flies in the face of Jeff's approach, because he would be the last to ascribe his "talents" (vis-à-vis interpreting the true meaning of dreams, and from there the long and difficult process of attempting to transform them for the benefit of himself, and the world at large) as a gift from any god, or gods. Such as it is, Jeff Lewis' battle is with those who would keep us asleep, in the dark, unaware of the possibility of controlling our own realities, whether in the dreaming or waking worlds. For Lewis, this is a psychic battle for the mind; one waged against the biblical gods of old, who through the ages have maintained a stranglehold upon our collective dreams and visions, both asleep and awake. While all of this might seem mere delusion to many of you reading these pages, it has been my experience that the significance of everyday events is influenced by occult symbolism and imagery, many of which come to us in the form of dreams.

It should be noted that it was only after receiving news of Keith's death that Jeff Lewis discovered the meaning of his "wounded knee" dream; a dream that apparently occurred at the same time that Keith suffered his knee injury. Afterwards--with news of his death--it became clear to Lewis that Jim's passing was associated to ancient Druid fertility rites, which, at their core, possessed "human sacrifice" underpinnings. Lewis' described this "sacrifice" of Jim Keith as one that would be accomplished "in a covert, unconscious fashion without apparent connection to the event or even conscious consent of the participants."

What is most astonishing is that these very themes (human sacrifice, fertility rites) were explored in the 1973 film, *The Wicker Man*, starring Christopher Lee. Although the creator of *Burning Man*, Larry Harvey, has never publicly acknowledged *The Wicker Man* as his inspiration, the connection between the two is undeniable, as anyone who has seen the movie--and has been to *Burning Man*--can attest. That Jeff Lewis was able to put these connections together--having never seen the movie or having been to *Burning Man*, for that matter--speaks to his ability to reach far into the subconscious realm of dreams, and make sense of the madness waiting there. In this case, the dream vision presented to Jeff was such that the "real" burning man *is* Jim Keith, who was sacrificed in deed, just as the "burning man" effigy is sacrificed each year at Black Rock Desert. Likewise, the lead character in *The Wicker Man* is similarly sacrificed to an effigy of a demon named King Wicker during his investigation of an occult group involved in pagan ritual sacrifice.

Jim Keith, due to his own investigations, such as the Casolaro affair and the Oklahoma Bombing, might have unwittingly set himself up for just this type of sacrifice. According to conspiratologist Michael Anthony Hoffman, *The Wicker Man* was also associated symbolically and alchemically to the Son of Sam murders, as outlined in Hoffman's treatise *Secret Societies and Psychological Warfare*. Quoting Hoffman: "The word wicker has many denotations and connotations one of which is 'to bend,' as in the 'bending' of reality. It is also connected to witchcraft through its derivative, wicca."

Although it would be a leap on my part to suggest that a deliberate plot was hatched along these lines (using the *Burning Man* festival and Washoe County Medical Center as a backdrop for the conspiratorial sacrifice of Jim Keith), I believe there may be other factors at work here, of an occult nature. Let it also be noted that Jim Keith is not the first casualty associated with *Burning Man*, as in 1996 another human was placed upon the symbolic sacrificial alter, the victim of a head-on motorcycle collision. Of course, that's not a bad track record when you consider how the event has grown over the years, and all the anarchic freedom unleashed there in a three-day span. *Burning Man*--for those not in-the-know--marked its humble beginnings back in 1986 at Baker Beach in San Francisco, when artist Larry Harvey, having just ended a troubled romantic relationship, built the first burning man, in a act of freeing himself from the past; a sort of banishment, and ritual working, from a love affair gone bad. The first "Man" was a mere eight feet tall, with twenty people in attendance for the burn. Twelve years later--at the last *Burning Man* I attended--the "Man" had grown to 50 feet tall, with approximately 15,000 people in attendance.

As logically fuzzy as this all may sound, I think Jeff Lewis is on to something here, and--for that matter--Michael Hoffman, as well, although there is a definite gulf between their two points of view. Hoffman's worldview subscribes to the theory that subliminal messages are being implanted on a subconscious level in the minds of modern man in order to usher in a New World Order. Conversely, Jeff Lewis feels that it is actually the subconscious realms that influence our conscious minds. So, in essence, a movie such as *The Wicker Man* is the outcome of conscious manipulation ala Hoffman, whereas in Jeff Lewis' worldview the realm of dreams influences such events as *Burning Man*, specifically in regards to Jim Keith's death. In this article, I have formed a bridge--albeit wobbly as all get-out--bringing these two divergent points together; at least for a brief instant, and perhaps shedding light on the alchemical and occult symbolism surrounding Jim Keith's death in relation to *Burning Man*.

As you may have gathered from my earlier thumbnail sketch of *Burning Man*, it's an event that needs to be experienced first hand to be grokked. Aside from one big free-for-all party and mindfuck, there are many levels going on at *Burning Man* in terms of human sacrifice--at least on an emotional, or psychic level--of opening one's self up to "spirit energies", in whatever form they may proceed. Oddly enough, I was crucified there myself. (A photo of this crucifixion appears in *SteamShovel Press* issue #18.)

Granted, I've had loads of fun at *Burning Man*, but yes, it's indeed a surreal spectacle infused with unbridled anarchy, not to mention people accidentally torching themselves, on occasion, during ritualistic "fire dances" in conjunction with the actual burning of the Man.

While putting this piece together, I sorted through my photo collection of *Burning Man* '97 and '98. What suddenly became evident was an undercurrent of human sacrifice, mixed in with such themes as fertility rites, sex magick workings, and occult symbolism. Like any risky venture in life, you definitely open yourself to unknown forces when you wander into any *Burning Man* event.

As I rooted through these photos of *Burning Man* past, there were a handful of shots that particularly stood out. One of note pictured yours truly inserting my head into one of the many orifices of a strange creation dubbed by its makers: "The Nebulous Entity", a many tentacled three-story tower. In a press release distributed by Nebulous Entity propagandists, this strange creation was described as that which "absorbs and metabolizes information." By day, The Nebulous Entity merely held its ground with nary a sound emitted from its arcane countenance, consisting of twirling appendages and the aforementioned purplish sucking orifices. That day, when I stuck my head into said orifice--out of sheer playfulness more than anything--I was not at all aware of the ulterior motives of this "Entity". Later, in revisiting this photo, the theme of human sacrifice once again reared its multifarious head, as I--in turn--had naively offered my own head on a platter to this strange "Nebulous Entity". After the ceremonial burning of "The Man" in 1998, the Ritual of The Nebulous Entity unfolded. By day, a mild manner sculpture, that night, illuminated from within--and playing the strangest music; a compilation of 50's atomic energy ditties, 70's bubblegum pop, and other twisted thrift shore treasures--The Nebulous Entity attracted a huge following of merry fools, all expecting to see it sacrificed in flames, just as "The Man" had been sacrificed before it. People were jumping and dancing and having a merry ol' time, as they followed "The Entity" across the Playa, attracted like moths to a flame in a crazy kinda conga line, mesmerized by these figurative Pipes of Pan. Though it all seemed like innocent merriment, occasionally the scene would get a bit eerie, as The Nebulous Entity would suddenly stop in its tracks, as the goofy music emanating from its surreal structure would likewise surcease. Strange violet lighting emanating from within the belly of this beast would then begin to pulse, as "The Entity" emitted sounds of such a nature as to give the effect that it was "consuming". Only later did it dawn on me what was going on. The music and spectacle was literally "sucking in" all spectators, as The Nebulous Entity was in reality feeding off the collective energy of the gathered throng, some 300 or so strong. Much of the aforementioned music played by "The Entity" was similar to the sort of propaganda muzak made popular in the 50's and 60's, a sort of Mickey Mouse Club atmosphere, with human beings inducted into something they thought was simple fun and frolic, while in reality there was a degree of insidiousness to the whole spectacle…Just the same, I wouldn't have missed it for all the world!

Kerouac's "CITYCitycity"

Having been a long time Kerouac devotee--and part-time Science Fiction enthusiast--I thought never the twain would meet, due to Kerouac's statement in his treatise, *Essentials of Spontaneous Prose*: "Modern bizarre structures (science fiction etc.) arise from language being dead, 'different' themes give illusion of 'new' life..."

It was Kerouac's contention that such artificial forms, i.e. Sci Fi, failed to capture the pure essence of speech; conversely, real themes taken from everyday life were more suitable vehicles for expressing the true voice of the Muse, much as jazz is the ideal framework for a saxophonist to 'blow'. This was how Kerouac saw the craft of writing, as a free-form improvisation--ala jazzman with sax--letting the subconscious mind blow mighty riffs of words on paper with stream of consciousness abandon.

Saith Saint Jack again in *Essentials of Spontaneous Prose*: "If possible write 'without consciousness in semi-trance' (as Yeats' later 'trance-writing'), allowing subconscious to admit in own uninhibited interesting necessary and so 'modern' language what conscious art would censor, and write excitedly, swiftly, with writing-or-typing-cramps, in accordance with laws of orgasm, Reich's 'beclouding of consciousness'..."

Kerouac's criticism of Science Fiction was, in essence, a critique of all literature that relies on artificial constructs and formula. Kerouac himself was liken unto jazzman blowing his horn to high heaven, letting the spontaneous muse flow, free from the strictures of "literary convention." To Jack, writing was a form of sexual release, as jazz was a similar form of communication, or like Neal Cassady behind the wheel of a car, letting the cosmic flow of life direct his crazy caterwauling course, making mad history in the process.

Once, while perusing various Kerouac biographies, I happened across a reference to a science fiction story Jack wrote called, "CITYCitycity", which came as a bit of a surprise, outlining--as it did--Kerouac's version of a totalitarian cyber-society set against the backdrop of a futuristic earth plagued by overpopulation and ruled by she-demon feminists. I thought: Jeez, Kerouac blowing a science fiction riff...Like, crazy!

According to Beat legend, around '55 Kerouac resumed work on "CITYCitycity", a "Sci-Fi story" he began sometime during the heyday of the McCarthy hearings. Originally, Jack sent a draft to his friend William S. Burroughs in the eventuality that the two could develop the story together into a satiric novel, though nothing ever came of this prospective collaboration.

"CITYCitycity" was later sold for a whopping fifty dollars to the New American Reader and subsequently published in *The Moderns: An Anthology of New Writing in America*, edited by Leroi Jones. However, my search for the story proved no easy task, though I eventually tracked down this anthology, which was located in only four libraries across the globe: two in Great Britain, and two in the U.S. Finally, I was able to borrow a copy from Kansas State University, and at last lay my eyes upon this unheralded masterpiece depicting a Brave New World overrun with Thought Police and wondrous drugs that numb the mind to--that dirty word--'Activism'. Writes Jack in "CITYCitycity":

> Activated...a word written in black letters dripping with red ink...ACTIVATED, you'd see written on superseptic toilet walls of the cityCityCITY, with lewd drawings. It was a word whispered in dark sex rooms, turned into a colloquial dirty-word Activate me.

In his Orwellian tale, Kerouac paints a stark picture of the 'antiseptic city', where such things as 'pockets' have been outlawed, thus limiting the dumbed-down citizenry from concealing anything on their bodies not authorized by the ruling faction. Mandatory drug ingestion and Multivision viewing are required for all inhabitants of cityCityCITY, as every "Deactivated person" is equipped with "Brow Multivision set, just a little rubber disc adhering to the brow." Multivision is Kerouac's version of Orwell's 'one eyed monster' staring into every living room and desiccated soul; much more far-reaching than mere TV, Multivision is the ultimate Cyberpunk nightmare, monitoring the lives of quiet desperation as they unfold on a planet where legalized murder is the only way to keep the population in check. As Jack explains the cityCityCITY method of population control:

> It was necessary at intervals to electrocute entire Zone Blocks and make room for a new group culled from slags and miscalculations in the system. Deactivation which prevented

people from leaving their own Zone Blocks, was a necessary caution against the chaos which would have resulted from an overpopulated Movement over the crowded steelplate of the world. Migrating to other planets was out of the question; especially after centuries of Self Enforced Deactivation. Other planets in the immediate vicinity of earth had been denuded of life and turned into Deactivator Bases and Laboratories, Deactivating all that part of the universe around the earth. Outside raged the life of the Universe, where Activation reigned. Many were the spaceships from unknown planets who'd come crashing against the No-Zone of earth and disintegrated in midair; many the meteors met the same fate. Nobody questioned the wisdom of Master Center Love in refusing to have any contact with the rest of the universe.

Viewed in conjunction with 'L'--the Love Drug--the breastbones of the mirthless cityCityCITY inhabitants are riveted with transmitters monitoring their brainwaves to insure that they're remaining in accordance with the messages--aired on Multivision--via Master Center Love, the central hub of this mass mind controlled society, Earth circa 2900 A.D. This breastplate disc also serves as a drug dispenser, keeping its users 'pumped' with 'L'.

Like novelist Henry Miller, Kerouac saw post-World War II America as an "air conditioned nightmare"; the freedom to be whatever one chose was rapidly diminishing during the reign of Eisenhower. Eventually, Kerouac felt, we would all become robotoids, totally controlled by government bureaucracies, and perhaps even told when to die, as envisioned in "CITYCitycity".

The story--"cityCityCITY"--centers around a day in the life of a lad named M-80, who one morning makes the most amazing discovery on the streets of cityCityCITY--that of a pool of water.

(M-80's) heart thumped. He had never seen a pool of water in his life, except in Multivision in their history shows, showing how, in the days before rain was diverted from cityCityCITY, moisture used to fall from the skies and form in the streets and blocks of old cities. "There's been a leak!" thought the kid frantically. "What'll they say? Wow!"

And with the discovery of this pool of the unexpected, a crack in the armor of uniformity and conformity has surfaced--no doubt caused by 'Activists!'--sending a ripple of wonderment and dread throughout cityCityCITY, that could only be squelched by way of state sanctioned euthanasia. For eons rain had been diverted by a giant umbrella of energy draped over cityCityCITY, of which:

> ...every inch was covered with electronical steelplate. The ocean had long ago been covered with earth acquired from surrounding planets. CITYCITYCITY was the world; every square inch of the world was covered with three types of Levels of CITYCITYCITY. You saw the skyline, of skyscrapers far away; then beyond that, like a ballooned imitation of the same skyline, rising way beyond and over it, vastly larger, the second level of CITYCITYCITY, the CITY level; beyond that CITY, like a dim cloud rose huge on the horizon a vast phantasmal skyline so far away you could barely see it, yet it rose far above the other two and far beyond. Those three levels were to facilitate the ingress of sunlight into the various people-flats. The CITYCITYCITY Tri-Levels were: one tenement ten miles high; the second, fifty miles; the third, a hundred miles high so that from Mars for instance, you saw the earth with its complete CITY everywhere looking like a prickly ball in the Void.

Coupled with Kerouac's Orwellian vision, there's also a paranormal element to the story, no doubt inspired to some degree by Kerouac's close association with Burroughs, whose slant on telepathic transmission via disembodied entities is clearly evident throughout "cityCityCITY":

> ...Ideas of Activation had been brought onto the earth-globe via the only form of Activated life in the universe that was capable of penetrating the Great Electronics wall: beings on a level of certain rarity that enabled them to swim, veil-like, pale as ghosts, through the Wall and through the people of earth, yet communicating thoughts and ideas. For a long time they were said to be Tathagatas from a Buddha-land...
>
> ...These Beings, these Activation Agents, were the terrors of the world; the troops of Devils of Gothic times were replaced by these pale phantasmal insinuators from Outside, called Actors. This name was referred philologically back to ancient times when disorderly elements were known as "actors"...

Adam Gorightly

Illicit Actor Fumes were sold in forbidden little jars; Actor Fumes came from the emanation which an Actor left when it passed thru a jar, apparently by intention; the sniff of it had the peculiar effect of inducing a certain blissful feeling that was accompanied by a vitamin lapse, or false recharge, that made it impossible to inject L. (Love, the official CITY CITYCITY drug, used by everyone from birth, by law); with the effect of actor fumes, a man of this world was left wide open for telepathic messages from Actors infesting the air; nothing Multivision could send out could combat this, once the victim had a sniff of Actor Fumes, or Ghost, as it was called; it was so powerful and so sweet to the senses the weaker elements of the population were all addicted; it was easy to get, the Actors saw to that, by merely passing themselves through every jar in the world; jars became illegal...

If--back in the mid-50's--you'd given Ray Bradbury a few good drags of some Lebanese blond, this is just the type of mind-bending tale that would have emerged.

Look for it at an interlibrary loan near you!

Ritual Magic, Mind Control and the UFO Phenomenon

Not long after my own encounter with strange aerial phenomena, I began to see a link between UFO's to such seemingly disparate topics as psychedelics, psychotronics, and ritual magick. As the years pass, the Extraterrestrial Hypothesis (ETH) makes far less sense to this observer than other theories ranging from mind control conspiracies, or--on the other hand--fissures in the space/time continuum which provide a portal of entry for ghostly apparitions that can be saucer-shaped or even take on the form of Moth-Men, Chupacabras or the Blessed Virgin Mary.

UFO's encompass a wide range of phenomena and cannot be categorized simply in terms of little grey skinned buggers from Zeta-Reticuli shoving probes up human rectums. (Ouch!) To me the term "UFO" simply suggests something unexplainable hovering in outer or inner space, whether it is machine-like elves encountered under the influence of DMT, or nuts and bolt craft performing inexplicable aerial maneuvers over Area 51.

UFO's are limited only by our imaginations, and to consider them merely craft from another galaxy is as narrow a view as postulating that newborn babes are delivered exclusively by storks. UFO's are also--in my estimation--a product of altered consciousness, which is not to suggest that all sightings are in part, or in whole, complete confabulations. What I'm suggesting is that in order to observe UFO's, one must often enter into a more receptive state, much like a psychic or channeler tuning into voices or subtle energies. Channelers must first induce in themselves a trance state before being able to contact 'voices from the beyond'. The same goes for magical workings wherein magicians carry out rituals in order to invoke spirits and/or demons.

A corollary to the above statement is the famed Amalantrah Working of legendary occultist Aleister Crowley, which consisted of a series of visions he received from January through March of 1918 via his then 'Scarlet Woman', Roddie Minor. Throughout his life, Crowley had a number of Scarlet Women who acted as 'Channels' for otherworldly transmissions of angelic and/or demonic origin. The Scarlet Woman also played a large part in Crowley's notorious sex rituals, at times combining drugs and bestiality to stir up those strange energies into which good ol' Uncle Al was trying to tap. To quote Crowley chronicler Kenneth Grant from *Aleister Crowley and the Hidden God*:

> Crowley was aware of the possibility of opening the spatial
> gateways and of admitting an extraterrestrial Current in the

human life-wave...It is an occult tradition--and Lovecraft gave it persistent utterance in his writings--that some transfinite and superhuman power is marshaling its forces with intent to invade and take possession of this planet... This is reminiscent of Charles Fort's dark hints about a secret society on earth already in contact with cosmic beings and, perhaps, preparing the way for their advent. Crowley dispels the aura of evil with which these authors (Lovecraft and Fort) invest the fact; he prefers to interpret it Thelemically, not as an attack upon human consciousness by an extra-terrestrial and alien entity but as an expansion of consciousness from within, to embrace other stars and to absorb their energies into a system that is thereby enriched and rendered truly cosmic by the process.

It was through the Amalantrah Working--which included the ingestion of hashish and mescaline in its rituals--that Crowley came into contact with an interdimensional entity named Lam, who by the way just happens to be a dead ringer for the popular conception of the 'Grey' alien depicted on the cover of Whitley Strieber's *Communion*. Crowley called them "Enochian entities" because he purportedly contacted them by using "Enochian calls", a Cabalistic system/language devised by 17th century Elizabethan magician, Dr. John Dee. From this alleged encounter, some have inferred that the industrious Mr. Crowley intentionally opened a portal of entry through the practice of ritual magick, which allowed the likes of Lam and other 'alien greys' a passageway onto the Earth plane. Dr. John Dee and his "scryer", Edward Kelly, had their own strange encounters with--as they called them--"little men" who moved about "in a little fiery cloud", thus a pattern exists in the lore of ritual magic connecting UFO's to sorcery.

Some now believe that what Crowley tapped into was the same cosmic current that helped launch the current rash of alien abductions, as reported by such UFO researchers as Bud Hopkins, John Mack, David Jacobs, et al. When making these connections, bear in mind that many abductees recall their encounters with these grey skinned creatures only after they've been hypnotically regressed. Once again, we see that trance states--not unlike those altered states of consciousness produced during rituals such as the Amalantrah Working--are often the triggering factor which opens up a portal for these strange entities. According to Kenneth Grant, this tradition has been continued by current day adepts of Crowley, who follow in his footsteps practicing ritual magic to invoke these "alien entities".

In *Outside the Circles of Time*, Grant writes:

> Some believe that the UFO phenomena are part of the "miracle", and a mounting mass of evidence seems to suggest that mysterious entities have been located within the earth's ambience for countless centuries and that more and more people are being born with innate ability to see, or in some way sense their presence....Prayer for deific intervention in ancient times has now became a *cri de coeur* to extra-terrestrial or interdimensional entities, according to whether the manifestations are viewed as occurring within man's consciousness, or outside himself in apparently objective but often-invisible entities. New Isis Lodge has in its archives the sigils of some of these entities. The sigils come from a grimoire of unknown origin which forms part of the dark quabalahs of Besqul, located by magicians in the Tunnel of Quliefi. The grimoire describes Four Gates of extraterrestrial entry into, and emergence from, the known Universe.

What Grant is speaking of is a form of ritual magick practiced by such groups as the Golden Dawn, and the Ordo Templi Orientis (O.T.O.). "Sigils" are line drawings and diagrams that serve as signatures of entities accessible to a trained magician familiar with "Enochian calls" and other methods of summoning "spirits". A grimoire is a directory of such sigils, and a manual for their use.

A noted disciple of Crowley's, Jack Parsons--one time head of the California branch of the O.T.O., and renowned rocket scientist--carried on this tradition of interdimensional contact when, in 1946--with the aid of "Frater H."--he made contact with some sort of entities not at all unlike Crowley's "Lam". This all took place during a series of magic rituals deemed The Babalon Workings. What makes this story all the more bizarre is that Parsons' accomplice in this endeavor--the aforementioned Frater H.--became more commonly known afterwards as charismatic cult leader L.Ron Hubbard, the founder of Scientology.

Apparently, Hubbard played a role similar to that of Edward Kelley, "scryer" for the aforementioned Dr. John Dee, of whom Crowley was an ardent admirer. A scryer works as a receptor of otherworldly communications, often using crystal ball or similar device in conjunction with the magician's rituals and ceremonies to summon beings from other dimensions. Together magician and scryer work left hand-in-hand in summoning these otherworldly beings: be they angels, demons or spirits of the dead. Crowley's Scarlet Woman, in many instances, performed this same function; for instance Crowley's first wife, Rose Kelly--while in a magical trance--received the first three chapters of the infamous *Book of the Law*, the manuscript that laid the foundation for Crowley's religion, Thelema. Furthermore, the portal of entry for the extraterrestrial beings that Crowley theoretically opened (when he invoked the entity "Lam") may have been further enlarged by Parsons and Hubbard with the commencement of the Babalon Working, thus facilitating a monumental paradigm shift in human consciousness. As Kenneth Grant wrote, "The [Babalon] Working began...just prior to the wave of unexplained aerial phenomena now recalled as the 'Great Flying Saucer Flap'. Parsons opened a door and something flew in." Such researchers as John Carter suggest that the detonation of atomic bombs over Japan--during the latter part of World War II--may have also played a part in opening this door between dimensions or, at the least, attracted the curiosity of our intergalactic neighbors.

As Thelemic history instructs, 1947 ended the first stage of the Babalon Working, as Parsons and Hubbard parted ways after a falling out. (Apparently, Hubbard ran off with Parsons' wife and a large part of his fortune.) It was the same year the Modern Age of UFO's began with the Kenneth Arnold sightings over Mt. Rainer in Washington State, followed not long after by the alleged saucer crash in Roswell, New Mexico.

1947 was also the year that marked the passing of The Great Beast, Aleister Crowley. Not long after these monumental events, in 1948, Albert Hoffman gave birth to LSD, which indicates that strange things were indeed afoot in the collective unconscious of humanity between the years of 1946-'48. Connecting all this high weirdness up even tighter is conspiracy researcher John Judge, who--in an interview on KPFK radio, Los Angeles on August 12, 1989 dubbed "Unidentified Fascist Observatories"--stated that Kenneth Arnold and Jack Parsons were flying partners, though I have, as yet, been unable to find additional corroboration to support this claim.

As for L. Ron Hubbard--though it is not well publicized by current day members of the Church of Scientology--much of his "religion" was based on a bizarre cosmology he apparently concocted, perhaps to see how much his flock was willing to swallow; a thesis which suggested that several million years ago the souls of dead space aliens (Thetans) entered into the body of Earth humans, and that is part of the reason why today we are so screwed up as a species.

Another interesting "UFO" parallel to note is that Parsons and Hubbard's visionary experience with these alien-like entities transpired in the California desert, which during the late 40's and 50's was a hotbed for flying saucer activity. It was in this setting that such famous "Contactees" as George Adamski and George Hunt Williamson invoked their own brand of cosmic messengers, transported by saucers, cigar-shaped vessels and the like, often originating for nearby Venus, or other seemingly uninhabitable planets in our solar system.

In the 1930's--prior to his "Space Brother" encounters--Adamski operated a monastery dubbed "The Royal Order of Tibet", which afforded him a permit to make sacrificial wine during the Prohibition. After the Prohibition ended, Adamski opened a burger stand near the Mount Palomar Observatory. While there, Adamski claimed to have helped astronomers photograph several UFO's-a claim that afterwards was never verified by anyone at the observatory.

Adamski's first encounter with the "Space Brothers" occurred in the Mojave Desert on November 20, 1952, when--in the company of George Hunt Williamson and some other friends--he witnessed a cigar-shaped craft being pursued by military jets. Just before disappearing from sight, the craft ejected a silver disc, which landed a short distance from Adamski and his party. When Adamski arrived at the saucer he was greeted by a man with long blond hair, wearing a one-piece suit. Telepathically, the "man" informed Adamski he was from Venus, and that he was concerned about the possibility of atomic bomb radiation from Earth reaching other planets in the solar system, and that various beings from throughout the galaxy were visiting Earth harboring these same concerns. According to Adamski, he was taken aboard one of the alien ships and flown around to several venues throughout the universe, including the dark side of the moon. During the course of his aerial foray, Adamski took an array of spurious photographs that have been widely viewed as a hoax. In "Unidentified Fascist Observatories" John Judge asserts that Adamski was an asset of the CIA, who in his lecture tours throughout the 50's and 60's dispersed disinfo on behalf of the Company.

Adamski's colleague--George Hunt Williamson--went on to author several UFO books, such as *Other Tongues--Other Flesh*, and promulgated the idea of a cosmic good-versus-evil battle taking place between the "good guys" from the dog star, Sirius, versus the evil shit-kickers from Orion. Strangely enough, the planet Sirius is a recurring theme found throughout occult and UFO lore.

Of note in this regard is Robert Temple's *The Sirius Mystery*, published in 1977, which documents the history of the Dogon tribe of Africa, and their fabled meetings with the Nommos, a race of three-eyed, crab-clawed beings from Sirius. It was these intergalactic emissaries--as Dogon legends record--that passed onto the tribe as far back as 3200 B.C. various astronomical data instructing them that Sirius had a companion star invisible to the naked eye. These legends far predate the advent of telescopes, and were later confirmed by astronomers. This "companion" star--Sirius B--wasn't even photographed until 1970. In addition to this knowledge regarding Sirius B, the Nommos also provided additional info to the Dogons; such as the fact that Jupiter has four moons, Saturn has a ring around it, and that the planets in our solar system orbit around the sun. All of these facts were later confirmed by science.

In *The Sirius Mystery*, Temple traces contact with the Nommos all the way back to Sumeria circa 4500 B.C. At that time, he says, these three-eyed-crab-clawed creatures appeared in their mighty space ships from the stars, bestowing unto humankind vast secrets; revealing mysteries and esoteric knowledge passed on to initiates in various secret societies in Egypt, the Near East, and Greece. These initial contacts, Temple contends, planted the seeds for the various mystery religions, whose offshoots include the likes of Giordano Bruno, Dr. John Dee, and the overall foundation which laid the stones for Freemasonry, and other secret schools of esoteric knowledge such as The Knights Templar and the Rosicrucians. In fact, Freemasons believe that civilization on Earth was initially formed by entities from the Sirius star system, whom they equate with the Egyptian Trinity of Isis, Osiris, and Horus. In these legends, Osiris has been portrayed as a precursor to Christ, who was first crucified then later resurrected, forming the basis of an Egyptian priesthood that worships Sun gods. The adepts of these mystery religions have always referred to themselves--in one form or another--as The Illuminati; those who have been "illuminated" by their worship of the various Sun gods/Moon goddesses.

In his treatise, Temple further notes that the entire Egyptian calendar revolved around the movements of Sirius, and that the calendar year began with the 'dog days' when Sirius started to rise behind the sun. According to Philip Vandenberg in *The Curse of the Pharaoh*: "An archeologist named Duncan MacNaughton discovered in 1932 that the long dark tunnels in the Great Pyramid of Cheops function as telescopes, making the stars visible even in the daytime.

The Greater Pyramid is oriented, according to MacNaughton, to give a view, from the King's Chamber, of the area of the southern sky in which Sirius moves throughout the year."

The brightest star in the heavens, Sirius is approximately 35 times brighter than our own sun, and is regarded in occult circles as the "hidden god of the cosmos". The famous emblem of the all-seeing eye, hovering above the unfinished pyramid, is a depiction of the Eye of Sirius, a common motif found throughout Masonic lore. It is no secret that many of our nation's founding fathers were Freemasons, which explains the odd appearance of the Eye of Sirius on the dollar bill; a symbol seen everyday by millions of people, imprinting its image forever in our psyches. The imprinting of such imagery has been called into question in recent times by a whole host of conspiracy theorists, who--in their New World Order scenarios--connect such fraternal orders as the Knights of Malta, Freemasonry and Rosicrucianism with the "insidious" symbol of Sirius, the eye in the triangle. At the top of this pyramid--the conspiracy theorists contend--is the dreaded Illuminati, tying all of these fraternal orders and secret societies together in a far flung plot intended to bring mankind to its knees under a futuristic Orwellian nightmare; a tolitarian society masquerading as a libertarian democracy, which uses Masonic imagery to program the masses.

And if this entire story wasn't already jumbled enough, the dawning of the 20th century ushered in a new generation of contactees paying homage to the "Dog Star", expounding ever further upon the legend of the hovering eye atop the pyramid. Right around the turn of the century, a gentleman named Lucien-Francois Jean-Maine formed an order in Haiti called the Cult of the Black Snake that used rituals borrowed from Crowley's O.T.O. in combination with certain voodoo practices. In 1922, these rituals reportedly summoned forth a disembodied being named Lam, the very same entity that Aleister Crowley made contact with a few years earlier. In fact, Kenneth Grant has stated that Crowley "unequivocally identifies his Holy Guardian Angel with Sothis (Sirius), or Set-Isis."

Later--in the 1950's and 60's--the aforementioned saucer "Contactee" George Hunt Williamson once again summoned forth certain denizens purportedly from Sirius, conversing to them in the same 'Enochian' or 'angelic' language used by Dr. John Dee and Aleister Crowley. Williamson--in his various books and lectures--also spoke of a secret society on Earth that has been in contact with Sirius for thousands of years, and that the emblem of this secret society is the eye of Horus, otherwise known as the all-seeing eye.

Ritual Magic, Mind Control, and the UFO
Phenomenon

As previously noted, Williamson was a close associate of George Adamski, perhaps the most famous of the early UFO Contactees, who claimed to be connected with astronomers at Palomar Observatory in California, in whose company he allegedly witnessed several UFO sightings. In an essay entitled "Sorcery, Sex, Assassination, and the Science of Symbolism", author James Shelby Downard describes a "Sirius-worship cult" reaching all the way to the highest levels of the CIA. In this provocative piece, Downard recounted one of their rituals taking place at the Palomar Observatory under the telescopically focused light of Sirius, bathing its participants in the luminance of the majestic Dog-Star.

A rash of Sirian references continued on into the 1970's, perhaps inspired by Robert Temple's book. In 1974, science fiction writer Phillip K. Dick had some sort of "mystical experience" which at first he attributed to psychotronic transmissions broadcast from Russia. According to Dick, these "micro-wave boosted telepathic transmissions," as he called them, commenced on March 20, 1974, showering him with streams of visual and audio data. Initially, this overpowering onslaught of messages that Dick received was extremely unpleasant and, as he termed them, "die messages". Within the following week, he reported being kept awake by "violet phosphene activity, eight hours uninterrupted." A description of this event in a fictionalized form appears in Dick's *A Scanner, Darkly*. The content of this phosphene activity was in the form of modern abstract graphics followed by Soviet music serenading his head, in addition to Russian names and words. Dick's original theory was that Russian mind control agents were targeting him with these transmissions.

At the outset, Dick felt the emanations invading his mind were of a malevolent nature, although in time he began to believe they were something entirely different. In a letter to Ira Einhorn dated February 10, 1978, Dick went into more depth on these psychotronic transmissions, claiming that they "seemed sentient". He felt that an alien life form existing in some upper layer of the Earth's atmosphere had been attracted by the Soviet psychotronic transmissions. Apparently, this alien life form operated as a "station", tapping into some sort of interplanetary communication grid that, "...contained and transmitted vast amounts of information."

What Dick initially received were the Soviet transmissions, but eventually this alien life form--whom he called Zebra--became "...attracted or potentiated by the Soviet micro-wave psychotronic transmissions." In the months that followed, this alien entity--according to Dick--vastly improved his mental and physical well being in a number of ways. It (Zebra) gave him "...complex and accurate information about myself and also about our infant son, which, Zebra said, had a critical and undiagnosed birth defect which required emergency and immediate surgery. My wife rushed our baby to the doctor and told the doctor what I had said (more precisely what Zebra had said to me) and the doctor discovered that it was so. Surgery was scheduled for the following day--i.e. as soon as possible. Our son would have died otherwise." (Dick's wife Tessa and others have since confirmed this story regarding the medical conditions of himself and son, Christopher.)

Phil Dick felt Zebra was totally benign, and it held great contempt for the Soviets and their psychotronic experiments. Furthermore, Zebra informed Dick that the Earth was dying, and that spray-cans were "...destroying the layer of atmosphere in which Zebra...existed."

It was not until several years after his "mystical experiences" with Zebra that Phil Dick finally wrote about these events in his classic novel *VALIS*. Prior to the publication of *VALIS*, Dick had never made any mention of Sirius in connection with the events that so drastically impacted his life. However, in this classic work, Dick renamed Zebra to VALIS (Vast Active Living Intelligence System) and identified it as a product of the Sirius star system, identifying its operators as three-eyed crab clawed beings.

During this same period--1973-74--Robert Anton Wilson was having his own experiences with "ET denizens" which at the time he thought were "telepathic communications from Sirius" as recounted in his mind-blowing book, *Cosmic Trigger*. Also in the early 70's, English mainstream novelist Doris Lessing began a series of Sci-Fi novels revolving around entities from Sirius, which was a definite departure from her previous literary offerings. In the third novel of this series, *The Sirian Experiments*, Lessing relates a tale with stunning similarities to Dick's VALIS experiences. When Robert Anton Wilson met Ms. Lessing in 1983, she said she had never read a lick of Dick--or Wilson, for that matter, so it's hard to tell how much of this was cross-pollination; be it intentional or a subconscious filtration process that leaked in and out of a few brains fixated on The Dog Star.

Another somewhat unlikely source for such conjecture was the heavy metal rock band Blue Oyster Cult. At face value, one might consider BOC another in a long line of head banging guitar slingers, but upon closer examination many of their lyrics allude to subjects occult and arcane, often referring to amphibian-like beings from outer space, as well as Sirius in their song "Astronomy": "...and don't forget my dog, fixed and consequent. Astronomy...a star!"

But not only has Sirius cropped up time and again in occult and UFO lore, but the ubiquitous Dog Star has also been mentioned in relation to certain mind control experiments which fall under the nefarious umbrella of the CIA's MKULTRA project. Purportedly started in 1953--under a program that was exempt from congressional oversight--MK-ULTRA agents and "spychiatrists" tested radiation, electric shock, microwaves, and electrode implants on unwitting subjects. The ultimate goal of MK-ULTRA was to create programmed assassins ala The Manchurian Candidate. The CIA also tested a wide range of drugs in the prospects of discovering the perfect chemical compound to control minds. LSD was one such drug that deeply interested CIA spychiatrists, so much so that in 1953 the Agency attempted to purchase the entire world supply of acid from Sandoz Laboratories in Switzerland. In fact, for many years the CIA was the principal source for LSD.

In recent years, various info on remote mind control technology has filtered into the conspiracy research community through such "alternative" publications such as *Full Disclosure, Resonance* as well as a Finnish gentleman by the name of Martti Koski and his booklet *My Life Depends On You*. Over the last decade, Mr. Koski has been sharing his horrifying tale, documenting as it does the discovery of rampant brain tampering committed upon himself and countless others. The perpetrators of these evil doings allegedly include the Royal Canadian Mounted Police, the CIA and Finnish Intelligence, among various other intelligence agencies. Where Sirius comes into the clouded picture is quite interesting: at one point during a mind control programming episode, the "doctors" operating on Koski identified themselves as "aliens from Sirius". Apparently, these "doctors" (or "spychiatrists") were attempting to plant a screen memory to conceal their true intentions. What this suggests is a theory that a handful of researchers-- namely Martin Cannon, Alex Constantine, David Emory and John Judge--started kicking around in the early 90's: that Alien Abductions were a cover for MK-ULTRA mind control shenanigans perpetrated by intelligence agency spooks.

According to Walter Bowart--in the revised edition of *Operation Mind Control*--one alleged mind control victim related an incident along these lines, purportedly occurring in the late 70's. In memories retrieved by hypnotic regression, it was revealed that the victim had been the recipient of a mock alien abduction, the intention of which

71

was to create a screen memory that would conceal the actual mind control programs enacted on the victim. The subject in this instance claimed to have seen a young child dressed in a small alien costume, similar in appearance to the aliens in Speilberg's *ET*. None of this, of course, dismisses outright the ETH; nor does it mean that ET's have never visited us. Nevertheless, its implications are staggering when one considers the impact and subsequent commercialization of the Alien Abduction Phenomenon, and how it has challenged and reshaped the belief systems and psyches of millions of the planet's inhabitants, in essence creating a new paradigm that prior to thirty years ago was virtually non-existent.

As chronicled in Bowart's *Operation Mind Control*, in the late 70's Congressman Charlie Rose (D-N.C) met with a Canadian inventor who had developed a helmet that simulated alternate states of consciousness, much like the virtual reality unit in the movie *Brainstorm*. One such virtual reality scenario played out by those who tried on this helmet was a mock alien abduction. Congressman Rose took part in these experiments, which consisted of this alien abduction scenario. Much to Rose's amazement, the simulated scenario seemed incredibly realistic. This device sounds quite similar to Dr. Michael Persinger's much-touted "Magic Helmet", which has been receiving a fair amount of press in recent years. Equipped with magnets that beam a low-level magnetic field at the temporal lobe, the "Magic Helmet" effects areas of brain associated with time distortions, and other altered states of consciousness. Although Bowart did not specifically name the inventor of the helmet in *Operation Mind Control*, chances are it was Persinger to whom he was referring. Persinger's name has also been bandied about by mind control researcher, Martin Cannon--in his treatise *The Controllers*--as a behind the scenes player in MK-ULTRA intelligence operations.

Persinger is a clinical neurophysicist and professor of neuroscience, whose work over the years has focused on the effects of electromagnetic fields upon biological organisms and human behavior. Persinger is an adherent to the theory that UFOs are the products of geomagnetic effects released from the Earth's crust under tectonic strain. His "Magic Helmet"--it has been noted--approximates the characteristics of Temporal Lobe Epilepsy (TLE) of which many an armchair theorist have attributed as being responsible for Phil Dick's VALIS experiences. One of the most common attributes of TLE are visions in the form of direct communications with God, or gods--in whatever form--be it aliens, angels, fairies or elves.

Early on--in his efforts to explain his own abduction experience--author Whitley Strieber entertained the possibility that he might have been one such victim of TLE. Because of this, Strieber underwent extensive medical examinations--including several CAT scans and MRI's--to determine if such was the case, but the results of all these tests came up negative. Aside from such speculations, there is an undeniable magical component to Whitley Strieber's experiences. After his initial hypnotic regression--when the presence of the "visitors" were first revealed to him--Strieber subsequently practiced a form of meditation to further conjure their image in his mind, so as to better identify their features. The first time he attempted this approach--much to his surprise--an alien grey immediately appeared in his "mental field of view", allowing Strieber to delve deeper into the mystery of the phenomenon. This meditation experience--as recounted in *Communion*--seems nothing less than a magical conjuration, although Strieber may not have been entirely aware of his actions in the context of ritual magic. In a sense, Strieber perhaps performed unconscious magical workings on several occasions, in essence summoning forth these beings from behind the veils of perception.

Furthermore, it is my belief that hypnotic regression can, under certain conditions, perform a sort of magical working, and it was through hypnotic regression that Strieber was able to come to terms with his "visitor experience". Bear in mind that hypnosis approximates a trance state, and it is just this form of altered consciousness that has allowed many an abductee to recall their experiences. Strieber was also, prior to his "visitor" experience, a member of the Gurdjieff Foundation, a self-transformational organization dedicated to a system of techniques devised by the famed mystic G.I. Gurdjieff. As Strieber explained: "I believe that the techniques I learned in that training--particularly a form of double-tone chanting--have enabled me to remain conscious in some experiences with the visitors where I otherwise would have been unconscious." What Strieber doesn't acknowledge is that Gurdjieff himself was in contact with certain denizens of Sirius via this method of double-tone chanting, which could also be describe as "Enochian chants."

It was in the early stages of his "visitor" experiences that Strieber made the acquaintance of famed alien abduction investigator Budd Hopkins, who sat in on some of Strieber's early hypnosis sessions. Later, when Strieber was working on the early drafts of *Body Terror* (the original working title of *Communion*) he sent Hopkins excerpts for comment. Hopkins--though he was convinced that Strieber had indeed been visited by alien beings--was somewhat distressed by the amount of high weirdness contained within the manuscript, although there were many parallels with other known abduction cases. During the course of some group abductee meetings attended by Hopkins, Strieber has been quoted as saying that "some people began volunteering stories about having left their bodies or other psychic experiences after their abductions. Budd wasn't interested in that, and would tell people to get back to talking about their abduction experiences. He refused to see a possible link between the experience of abduction and some kind of spiritual or psychic awakening happening in the people to whom experiences occurred."

Elsewhere in *Communion*, Strieber points out that the mental state produced by his encounters with the "visitors" could be approximated by a rare drug called Tetradotoxin, which in small doses causes external anesthesia, and in larger doses may bring about out of body experiences. Even greater doses of the drug can simulate near death experiences. According to Strieber, Tetradotoxin is the core of the zombie poisons of Haiti. What he doesn't mention is that Tetradotoxin was just one in a vast number of psychoactive compounds utilized by the CIA for their infamous MK-ULTRA mind control experiments. Throughout *Communion*, Strieber makes veiled references to mind control (of the MK-ULTRA variety.) At one point in the narrative--as Strieber is haphazardly tossing around various theories regarding his abduction experiences--he brings up the possibility that the alien greys may not have been actually using mental telepathy to communicate, but that something of a more technical nature might have been occurring, such as extra-low-frequency waves beamed into Strieber's brain, thereby producing the requisite "voices in his head".

Along these lines, Strieber adds the interesting aside "that the earth itself generates a good deal of ELF in the 1 to 30 hertz range. Perhaps there are natural conditions that trigger a response in the brain which brings about what is essentially a psychological experience of a rare and powerful kind. Maybe we have a relationship with our own planet that we do not understand at all, and the old gods, the fairy, and the modern visitors are side effects of it." Part of the appeal of *Communion* and subsequent books were, in my opinion, Strieber's ability to entertain a whole host of theories, and in the process open the reader's eyes to the various possibilities attempting to explain the UFO phenomenon, from fairy lore or travelers from alternate dimensions, to the very real possibility of some sort of ELF wave/mind control machine being responsible for his haunted reveries.

Excerpt from "UFO's, LSD and Me"

(An Unsent Letter to Jenny Randles)

12-12-86
Dear Ms. Randles,

I would like to relate an experience that happened to myself and a colleague in 1979 in Fresno, CA. Let me preface this statement by saying that we were under the influence of the hallucinogenic drug, LSD. But hear me out: these are not the ravings of a drug-saturated fruitcake; I am not an habitual drug user, nor have I used LSD for several years. But to deny that I was not under its influence when this incident occurred would be to give an incomplete account of what transpired on that fateful night.

On the night in question—fully under the influence of said drug—we observed several 'flying saucers', in several shapes, sizes and multicolored variations. I am not denying that what we saw were hallucinations, but if they were, then they were 'dual hallucinations', for we both saw the same sights and sounds.

Now, a brief description of this event: The sighting occurred along a levee located in a residential section of town. Before we arrived at the levee (we were on foot) we joked to ourselves about how we might see a UFO during our little 'trip'. We laughed to ourselves (somewhat uncontrollably) how no one would ever believe us due to the condition we were in. Anyway, after walking a short time on the levee, we saw our first 'UFO'. The sight of this made me fall to one knee and we were both astounded by its sight. During the course of the night we saw several, anywhere from six to eight. One was cigar shaped, some saucer shaped, one with a multi-colored propeller. This all occurred in the span of not more than an hour and a half, I think, though the passing of time was hard to estimate due to the effects of the drug.

The last one we saw appeared like a falling star in the sky that seemed to stop in mid-descent, then turned into a space ship, or whatever it was. After the sighting of this 'UFO' we turned around and headed back, the way we came.

Now I realize the descriptions I am giving are sketchy, but in retrospect it seemed almost like a dream, everything happening so fast.

Adam Gorightly

If I were to describe every little detail, I'd be here all night. So I'll try to wrap it up and sum up the experience in a few more words.

When we arrived back at the point where we saw the first UFO, a beam of light shot down directly in front of us some 50 yards away, emanating from nothing we could see. I said, "Wow, did you see that?" and my colleague responded that he saw it, too. Of course, we said things like, "Wow, did you see that?" and, "Oh, my God!" many times that night. Through the whole experience, we felt a presence communicating non-verbally to us. Obviously, we were the only ones who saw 'them'. There were many houses in the vicinity, with many people living there who could have seen 'them', but it appears that 'they' were for our eyes only. Perhaps 'they' were hallucinations, but if they were, it was a 'dual hallucination', for we both saw the same thing.

If you get the chance, write me and comment upon these 'dual hallucinations'.

P.S. Enjoyed your book, *Beyond Explanation* very much.

Human Stew

UFOs are coming
From another space & time
Traveling 'cross the Universe
To mutilate our minds
I've seen them in my visions
And on my TV screen
These evil genius aliens
In their space-age machines.

They call me on the telephone
Via telepathy
And tell me that they've come to Earth
To rule humanity
We're gonna have to stop them
Before it is too late
And we become their human toys
Mass slavery our fate.

So the time is nigh, my friends
It's clear what we must do
We must either blow our planet up
Or become human stew
For what's the use of living
Under whips and chains
Wielded by green masters
With huge mutated brains?

So now you know the story
Tell me what you're gonna do
Nuke this crazy planet
Or become human stew?
For what's the use of living
Once they mutilate your mind?
These evil genius aliens
From another space & time.

Tales from the Astral Plane

From the ages 18 to 20, I experienced, on several occasions, a strange sensation within the realms of sleep. Lying in bed, I would seemingly awaken--although in reality I was still deep asleep--as an electrical current shot through my slumbering body. In shock then my mouth would freeze open in lockjaw horror, as a tingling sensation of pins and needles began to creep across my body, and then soon after I would be jolted awake by the electrical/lockjaw horror of my uncommon dreams.

This occurred with regularity for several months, and I didn't enjoy it one bit. It was frightening, and in the throes of these strange dreams I felt as if an alien influence was trying to take possession of my body for some unspeakable reason of evil.

During this period, I took a trip down to southern California with my good friend Brian, and while there stopped over in Ventura to visit our mutual friend, MaryJane who, at the time, was working at Camarillo State Mental Hospital as a psychiatric social worker. A survivor of the 60's, MaryJane evolved as a radical free-thinking feminist through the 70's, along the way delving into drug experimentation, mysticism and various forms of mind expansion.

MaryJane's house was situated on a hillside, with a five-acre avocado orchard as a backyard. Though the house was quaint and comfortable--with semi-hippie furnishings and eclectic artwork--MaryJane felt ill at ease there. To find out why, one night MaryJane brought home one of her patients, a "sensitive" whom she was treating at Camirillo. The "sensitive" confirmed MaryJane's worst suspicions: that the house was haunted. (But that's another story.)

One night--after consuming a couple bottles of wine and waxing philosophical on the various meanings of life--I described to MaryJane the dreams I'd been having of the electrical current lockjaw variety. Instantly, her eyes lit up in recognition, as she grokked the higher plane my head was spinning on. "You've been astral projecting, Adam!" MaryJane dramatically announced.

Previously, I'd never connected these apparent dream experiences with astral projection. Now it started to make sense. MaryJane explained to me (as she understood the phenomena from her own experience and research) that what was happening with this electrical current, lockjaw and numbing sensation was the effect of my astral/spirit body leaving my mortal shell, its psychic energy causing an electric surge to course through me, freezing my jaw open in its passing, sending a wave of numbness through my supine frame as the psychic energy shot out of my human shell, in search of higher ground.

In the past I'd read here and there about astral projection in Castaneda's books, and in the teachings of ECKANKAR. Both seemed pretty far removed from me, and I never related them to my own personal experiences because I didn't realize what was happening. (Much like my earlier UFO experience, I don't know if what occurred to me during those spacey days was real or imagined.)

"Astral projection," I responded, astounded. "How do you know that's what's happening to me?"

"Because, my dear Adam, the same thing has been happening to me for years."

"Oh," I said, awaiting further clarification.

"Yes. I've been going through the same thing for years. Perhaps you're at the point now where you haven't left your body. It sounds as if your astral body is just about to leave your physical body, when you're jolted awake.

"Now, regarding myself...Well, it's pretty strange," MaryJane continued. "What happens is that--once I leave my human body--I am transported to some other world where I inhabit the body of this monster who runs 'round and 'round in circles, never getting anywhere. Round and round and round. I'm still trying to figure that one out."

"Wow, that's a trip."

From this point forward my wanderings within the astral plane started getting weirder and more productive. I don't know if this was from the fuel MaryJane had fed my ever-expansive imagination, or if I was progressing upon the path of wisdom to higher states that the guru-guys of old had mastered. In talking to my friend Jonathan H. about my astral wanderings, he related a passage to me from the Castaneda books where Don Juan told Carlos that one of the first steps of mastering control over your astral body was to be able--once out of body--to gaze down upon your sleeping shell where it rested on its earthbound bed. This then became my quest, yet every time I started astral projecting I could never remember to do it, because once in that state you move to a different level where you are no longer Adam Gorightly, but you become a sort of pure spirit energy, rising from the prison of our corrupted physical bodies into the ethers of the astral plane. But enough rambling. Let's get on with the actual descriptions of these astral experiences.

One of the first astral experiences I had, after discussing the phenomena with MaryJane, had me rising from bed, still in the supine position, my astral body levitating, three feet or so above my bed. After a short duration, I was thrust once again back into physical consciousness, which always seemed to me like a slingshot effect, my spirit flung back into the sleeping hull, physical awareness jerking it awake violently from its psychic slumbers.

When in these astral states, my spirit body would zoom around at incredible speeds, making right angle turns as it traveled at warp drive, around the walls and beneath the ceiling of my room. But never once did my astral body leave the room; it would just soar around in speedy circles, like some sort of caged and deranged metaphysical bird, searching for a passage to the sky.

Some of my final astral projection experiences were truly horrifying. After leaving my body, I began hearing voices as I floated around the room; the laughing haunting rumbling deep satanic voices of demons. I would awake from these experiences in a cold sweat, thinking my soul possessed by unclean spirits from the lower reaches of the astral plane. It was at this point that I made a conscious effort to cease with this astral madness, and soon after I never projected astrally projected again. Amen!

The Manson Family and the Beatles

(An excerpt from *The Shadow Over Santa Susana: Black Magic, Mind Control and the "Manson Family" Mythos*)

I think it's a subconscious thing. I don't know whether they did it or not. But it's there. It's an association in the subconscious. This music is bringing on the revolution, the organized overthrow of the Establishment. The Beatles know in the sense that the subconscious knows. –
Charles Manson

It was another ceremony around the campfire at Barker Ranch, like so many before in the high desert, or at Spahn Ranch. Charlie had just returned from his Los Angeles trip with Beach Boy Dennis Wilson and record producer Greg Jakobson, and the worm was turning in a strange new direction. All the peace and love vibes that had once been Manson's calling card were gradually dissolving, more and more each day, and in their place paranoia was oozing in--at steadily increasing doses--warning of impending disaster just around the bend. A large part of Charlie's inspiration for this sudden mood swing could be attributed to The Beatles' *White Album,* of which he spoke about in solemn tones around the campfire, which reflected intensely in his eyes.

> Are you hep to what the Beatles are saying?...They're telling it like it is. They know what's happening in the city; blackie is getting ready. They put the revolution to music...it's 'Helter-Skelter.' Helter-Skelter is coming down. Hey, their album is getting the young love ready, man, building up steam. Our album is going to pop the cork right out of the bottle.

Although growing steadily more paranoid about the general state of the world, Charlie's optimism about his recording career had been renewed by his recent trip into the city, and the release of the Beach Boys "Never Learn Not To Love" that Charlie had written the lyrics to. Paul Watkins--in his Tate/LaBianca testimony--gave his own spin on the Manson Family mindset during this period:

> Our music was going to lure Whitey's daughters to the desert, away from Haight Ashbury. Blackie would have no other means of releasing his tensions, so would turn to the white establishment. The murders were going to start in rich places like Bel Air and Beverly Hills in the summer of 1969. The super-atrocious crimes would disturb the rich piggies; the spades would scare Whitey. They'd go to the ghetto and shoot the garbage man and the Uncle Toms. The Black Muslims would be in hiding. The whites would split up the middle, some saying, 'Look at the things you are doing to the blacks!' The whites would kill each other off. Then the Black Muslims would come in and kill the rest of them. Helter Skelter is the end of the cycle. What was on top had to go on

the bottom. The karma of the whites is over and the black's karma begins. But then Revolution 9 takes over. This is described in Revelation 9. The black man would have to clean up the mess the white had made of the world, rebuild the cities and all that. But Blackie can't do it all alone. He will have completed *his* karma, and he'll have to come to the 'family.' Charlie will pat his fuzzy head and kick him. Charlie will have to show him how. Meanwhile, the 'family' will have grown to 144,000 like the twelve tribes of Israel in Revelation. Charlie encourages the girls to get pregnant. And we'll have buses to collect all the children when Helter Skelter comes down, so we can save them and raise them in our hole in the desert. The bottomless Pit. That's in Revelation 9, too...Charlie's mission is to complete the karma of the world.

Throughout late '68 and early '69, Manson Family members were spread throughout Death Valley, Topanga Canyon, Laurel Canyon, and one or more in England, allegedly with The Process Church of the Final Judgment. One former Manson Family associate claims that four to six members of the group lived on Laurel Canyon Boulevard in a log cabin once owned by actor Tom Mix. In Manson's famous letter to the *Hollywood Star*, he reminisced about the Tom Mix house:

We had a pool full of naked beauties and strobe lights in the living room & sex in 5 bedrooms & all the closets had secret doors that go from bedroom to bedroom plus guest house, big beds, pool shacks, and mattresses in the living room, a tree house, sex all over the grounds, in the rose gardens, under the trees. NEIL DIAMOND used to come over. MIKE LOVE, of the Beach Boys, DORIS DAY's son, ANGELA LANSBURY's daughter Dee Dee, NANCY, SINATRA's daughter, used to be at the beach pad.

We All Live In A Yellow Submarine

Around this time, Charlie and gang moved into a house at 21019 Gresham Street in Canoga Park, less than twenty minutes from Spahn Ranch. The house, made of stucco and redwood, was painted a bright canary yellow, and soon became known in Family lore as "The Yellow Submarine." From there, Charlie said, the Family would remain "submerged beneath the awareness of the outside world" while working on their music. The property itself sat on an acre of ground, with four bedrooms, two baths, a big kitchen and a large front room that was used as studio for Family recording sessions.

According to Charlie in *Manson In His Own Words*, within four weeks of moving into the Yellow Submarine, it had become a "concert hall for musicians, a porno studio for kinky producers, a dope pad, a thieves' lair, a place to dismantle stolen cars and just about everything but a whorehouse."

About a week or so after they moved into The Yellow Submarine, Charlie sent a squad back to Barker Ranch to retrieve Brooks Posten, Juanita Wildebush and Gypsy Share, the remaining Family members who had stayed behind to look after things. Around this time, two new girls joined the fold: Crazy Patty, a petite hippie chick from Canoga Park, and seventeen year old Barbara Hoyt, a buxom brunette, who would soon change her name to Bo Rosenberg.

The legendary "Death Mockup Party" was a prime example of the mounting weirdness that began to take hold during the Gresham Street period. They were all sitting around stoned in the middle of the living room one night, apparently postulating their own deaths, when Charlie--strategically positioned in the midst of the gathering--said, "Die," so they all laid down and pretended to die, goodbye. Bo started screamin' "Charlie", and then "Oh-h-h-h-h!" In response, Manson started moving his fingers about in strange reptilian patterns, talking about the confusion in the air, and how groovy it all was.

Meanwhile, Brooks had gone into a deep trance, and Charlie commanded him to shed his mortal coil. Brooks immediately died in his own mind, and stayed in this "Death Trance" for a total of five days. As he lay wasting away on the living room couch, the girls would periodically clean up after his natural bodily functions. On the fifth day of Brook's death, Charlie commanded that his very own ceremonial vest be placed beneath the ego-dead disciple as a sort of symbolic diaper, and with this one humble messianic act, Charlie was able to resurrect Brooks back to the world of the living, just like Jesus in the

Bible awoke Lazarus. Charlie looked down upon Brooks and said, "I command you to live again!" With Charlie's commandment, Brooks' eyes opened, as slowly and painfully he rose to his feet. Saith Charlie then: "Now I accept you."

Charlie's Music Career

Shortly after moving into the Gresham Street pad, the Family was paid a visit by Dennis Wilson and Greg Jakobson, who--after hearing Charlie and the gang play a few tunes--were enthused about the new "desert music." Because of this, Dennis, Jakobson and Melcher scheduled a couple recording sessions, the first one at a studio in Westwood Village.

When Charlie went to the studio for the first session, he brought the whole mob with him--about fifteen all told--invading the place like some sort of hippie free-for-all. Right away the guy who ran the studio started telling Charlie and his gang what they could and couldn't do; where to sit, where to stand, which way to face, even how to hold the microphone. At first, they complied with the studio manager's requests, but when it came time for Manson to lay down his vocals, the girls wanted to be looking at him when they sang background. As the girls started moving away from the place where they'd been positioned, the studio manager came unglued.

In the end, the scene was a repeat performance of what went down at previous recording sessions, as Charlie felt the studio wouldn't let him perform his music the way he wanted to, free from the restraints and deadlines of studio managers and record producers pushing their trip on him. Nevertheless, Manson managed to record about a dozen songs, two of which were spontaneously composed. It was at this session that Manson freaked-out Terry Melcher with a little spontaneous ditty of guitar vamp and scat-singing of apparently non-sense syllables "digh-tu-dai, deigh-du-doi, di-tew-deigh" which gradually became clearer until "di-tew-deigh, die-tew-dai," became "die today, die today, die today."

Much has been made about Charlie's aborted music career. Some suggest his failure to "hit the big time" was the main motive behind the Tate murders; that Charlie felt spurned by Terry Melcher, and in retaliation sent his shock troops to 10050 Cielo Drive to even the score. Manson scoffs at such accusations, insisting that his musical career was never of great importance to him.

The Hollywood S&M Scene

Charlie and the girls soon found themselves invited to private parties in Beverly Hills, Malibu and other exclusive areas. Until getting mixed-up with the Hollywood set, they had not been involved with kinky orgies featuring performances a la whips and chains but somehow they were drawn into it by this depraved Hollywood crowd, besot with loose morals and hard drug habits. It's interesting to note that whenever Charlie talks about this S&M scene, there is a certain amount of bitterness in his tone, indicating that something ugly might have gone down during this period. The Manson Family/Hollywood connections ran deep, and for many years Charlie was reticent to finger the rich and famous that had intersected his star-crossed path.

Manson decided to lift the lid on this "area of silence" when he responded to a request from a gossip tabloid in the mid-70's, *The Hollywood Star.* Among the "big names" that Charlie named were Elvis, Neil Diamond, various members of The Beach Boys, Nancy Sinatra, Jane Fonda, Yul Brynner, Peter Sellers and Peter Falk. When Frank Sinatra caught wind that the publisher of *The Hollywood Star*-- Bill Dakota--was calling his daughter Nancy to pump her for info regarding alleged Manson sex orgies, the "Chairman of the Board" threatened to send out some of his boys to break Dakota's knee-caps if the publisher didn't cease and desist.

According to Terry Melcher in *Doris Day: Her Own Story,* one persistent rumor surrounding the Tate/LaBianca murders was that Sebring lured some of Charlie's girls into one of the sado-porno films that he and his Hollywood friends were making, whipping and beating them before the camera. It doesn't take an overwhelming leap to entertain the possibility that all of this kinky weirdness might have led to the murderous rituals that unfolded during the hot August nights of 1969.

Sammy Goes Satanic

In his autobiography, *Why Me?*, Sammy Davis, Jr. recounted a party he attended in the late 60's, which turned out to be a orgy highlighted by a simulated virgin sacrifice. To his surprise, Davis discovered that the hooded man acting as the leader of the coven was none other than Jay Sebring, who-

-as Davis put it--had always been "a little weird." Sebring had constructed a dungeon in his basement and tried unsuccessfully to entice Davis over to view the "antique pieces" (torture weapons) he had collected. Shortly after the party, Davis met Anton LaVey, who warned him not to get involved in the Church of Satan unless he was serious about the commitment. Davis, while not totally serious, joined anyway because he "wanted to have every human experience" possible.

In his Vegas nightclub act, Sammy openly flaunted one symbolic red fingernail, and wore a Church of Satan Baphomet pendant around his neck. "The chicks loved it," playboy swinger Sammy noted, a smoke dangling from his lips. At one point, things started getting even too weird for Sammy-baby. "One morning after a 'coven' that wasn't quite fun and games," he recalled, "I got some nail polish remover and took off the red fingernail."

Adam Gorightly

Neil Diamond Stole My Chops

Manson claims to have met and influenced many of the movers and shakers of the 60's music industry. Among those whom Manson says "stole his chops" were The Beach Boys, Neil Diamond, and The Buffalo Springfield. According to Family member Sandy Good, former Springfield member Neil Young was amazed at Charlie's rhythmic style of playing, and supposedly gave Manson a motorcycle. Young's song "Mansion on The Hill" from *Ragged Glory* has long been rumored to be about his meeting with Charlie in the 60's. (i.e. "Manson on the Hill"): "His words were kind but his eyes were wild, he said 'I got a load to lug but I want one more trial'". Another Manson influenced tune by Mr. Young is "Revolution Blues." Young--who met Manson through Dennis Wilson--has been quoted as saying:

> He wanted to make records. He wanted me to introduce him to Mo Ostin at Reprise. He had this kind of music that nobody else was doing. He would sit down with a guitar and start playing and making up stuff, different every time, it just kept on comin' out, comin' out, comin' out. Then he would stop and you would never hear that one again....Musically, I thought he was very unique. I thought he really had something crazy, something great. He was like a living poet.

Operation Helter Skelter

During the Yellow Submarine period, Manson began recruiting former prison buddies and outlaw bikers and mechanics to help him score and repair dune buggies and Harleys. From his experiences in the rough and rugged terrain of Death Valley, Manson decided that dune buggies best fit the bill for the Family's envisioned mass exodus into the desert, as they were great for outrunning the pigs, and were light enough so that two or three Family members could lift them over impassable boulders and gullies. Manson would later outfit his sacred dune buggies with huge gas tanks, giving them a 1000 mile distance capability, and even put on machine gun mounts in preparation for Revelation. Charlie's own personal buggy was adorned with hanks of human hair, affixed to the roll-bar, donated by all the female Family members.

One of Charlie's ex-con recruits was Bill Vance (aka David Lee Hamic), who Charlie once recalled had a different name each time he met him. Vance was a hulking six-footer in his late 40's, with a battered face and a nose that looked like a craggy mountain range. He had been heavyweight champion of Brushy Mountain Prison, in Tennessee, one of the roughest prisons in the U.S., for nine years, which was some kind of record. They hit it off immediately, and Charlie used this liaison to further his own ends.

On March 23rd, 1969, Family member Bobby Beausoleil signed a songwriting contract with the Gerard Theatrical Agency on Sunset Strip. Beausoleil was given a key to the front door of the agency, and was allowed to use the tape recording equipment there to produce a demo. During that spring, Beausoleil had cultivated a relationship with Dennis Wilson, Terry Melcher and Gregg Jakobson, with designs of furthering his musical career. In fact, Jakobson went twice to the Gerard Agency to listen to Bobby's tapes, and in April, Bobby stayed for about a week at Jakobson's house on North Beverly Glen.

There he met and later lived with seventeen year old Kitty Lutesinger. In late May of '69, Kitty became pregnant courtesy of Beausoleil, and moved to Spahn Ranch just in time to see Helter Skelter coming down fast. Beausoleil also approached Frank Zappa, asking him to come out to the ranch to hear the Family's music, but Zappa declined. Apparently, Zappa and Beausoleil had formed a loose relationship during the early days of the Haight Ashbury, and Bobby had even performed a cameo on Zappa's first album, *Freak-Out* as one of the people in the background of a song yelling: "We are the brain police!"

The Gerard Agency specialized in supplying actors and actresses for porno flicks, and topless dancers for nightclubs. After hearing Bobby talk about the agency, Bill Vance--acting as "agent" for Sadie, Yeller, Stephanie, Katie, and Mary--was able to secure employment for the Manson girls as dancers at strip joints in the valley. Charlie encouraged them to take the jobs in order to buy vehicles and other supplies for their grand return to the desert. Former Family associate Allen "Fats" Walts, who used to roam the streets with Charlie while the girls danced and panhandled to support their messiah, claims that he and Manson often visited the home of Dean Martin, and that "Charlie delivered drugs there."

During this same period, Charlie and some of his girls made a porno movie by a swimming pool at the Malibu property of a Mrs. Gibson. The producer, according to Los Angeles homicide officers, was a guy named Marvin Miller. Mrs. Gibson, after receiving numerous complaints from her neighbors, inspected her house in the company of a lawyer and discovered a bloody machete, which police said Manson used to slash somebody's arm during the course of the filmmaking.

Karate Dave, a twenty-six year old Vietnam vet, was another heavy-duty recruit who hooked up with the Family during the Yellow Submarine period, and lived in a tree house in the backyard with Bo Rosenberg. It was through Dave and Bill Vance that other outlaw types were enlisted to help the Family prepare for Operation Helter-Skelter. These were guys who could score motor parts, camping gear and building supplies, and who would later work around the clock on various projects at Spahn Ranch. As the months passed, preparations for Helter Skelter accelerated, and though Manson rarely allowed this fringe biker and ex-con element into the inner circle of the Family, he was able to keep them around through enticements of dope and sex.

One favorite trick of Charlie's was the strip and suck command. Executed with a wave of the hand, Manson would have his girls undress and go down on the bikers, which they no doubt got a big kick out of.

By the middle of March, the Family had acquired three dune buggies and three Harleys. In addition, Charlie bought three hundred dollars worth of topo maps so that they could chart an escape into the desert. The escape route began behind Spahn Ranch, up into the Santa Susana Mountains by way of Devil's Canyon, and ran through Simi Valley, bypassing highways, going over and under culverts, across the Mojave Desert and eventually leading them out to Death Valley. This clandestine route was to be used at the time of Helter Skelter, when everything was going crazy in the cities--and the highways leading out of L.A. would be in violent gridlock--an escape route that would be a quick exit away from the chaos.

The Fab Four Angels

According to Paul Watkins in *My Life With Charles Manson*, it was at the Gresham Street pad that Charlie really started getting heavy into the Beatles, particularly *The White Album*, which he interpreted as modern day prophecy, and the Beatles themselves as messengers of the Apocalypse retitled Helter Skelter. Charlie spent endless hours quoting Revelation to the Family, specifically the verse from chapter 9:

And the four angels were loosed
Which were prepared for an hour
And a day, and a month, and a year,
For to slay the third part of man
And the fifth angel sounded,
And I saw a star fall from heaven
Unto the earth: and to him was
Given the key to the bottomless pit.

For those with ears to hear, the implications were quite clear: the four angels were the Beatles, and the fifth angel was Charlie! The "third part of man" was the white race; those who would die in the resultant carnage of Helter Skelter, wiped out for "worship of idols of gold, silver, bronze, stone and wood," (Verse 20) which Charlie related to cars, houses, and money; those modern idols worshipped by the piggies.

The passage: "And he opened the bottomless pit...and there came out of the smoke locusts upon the earth; and unto them was given power as the scorpions of the earth have power" was not only a reference to the Beatles (i.e. locusts) but also implied that the power of the scorpion would prevail. (Charlie was a Scorpio.) Manson found references to dune buggies, as well as the motorcycle gangs he was trying to recruit, in such passages as "horses prepared to battle" and horseman that would roam the earth, spreading destruction.

In describing the locusts (Beatles), Revelation said that "their faces were as the faces of men," yet "they had the hair of women," and wore "breastplates of fire," which Charlie interpreted as electric guitars. Another verse from Revelation spoke of "fire and brimstone" coming from the mouths of the four angels, which Charlie interpreted as an allusion to the power of The Beatles' music and lyrics. Some have suggested that it really wasn't Charlie who invented Helter Skelter, but that he just became hip to the concept through channeled messages via the Beatles. Other apocalyptically inclined cults in California of the period held similar beliefs regarding an impending eschatological disaster, so the Family was not unique in this respect.

The White Album

In the same manner that Manson became a self-styled student of the Bible, likewise he threw himself into interpreting *The White Album*, which he listened to with headphones as a means to decipher the messages hidden in the vinyl grooves. Soon, it has been suggested, Manson began to hear the Beatles whispering to him: "Charlie, Charlie, send us a telegram." on the song "Revolution #9." At one point, Manson actually tried to call The Beatles in London, but was unsuccessful contacting them.

The White Album became such an influence upon the Family that various expressions from Beatles lyrics punctuated their speech. It was all there, Charlie would tell them; just listen to the music. Didn't they have a song called "Sexy Sadie" that described Susan Atkins to a tee, not long after Charlie himself had christened her Sadie Mae Glutz? Didn't the Beatles tell blackie it was time for them to rise up when they sang "Blackbird singing in the dead of night...All your life, you were only waiting for this moment to arise"? Not only that, but according to Charlie, the Beatles knew that he was out in Los Angeles, and were urging him to speak out, to sing the truth to the world, in their song "Honey Pie": "Oh honey pie, my position is tragic, come and show me the magic of your Hollywood song." In "Honey Pie", the Beatles even went so far as to beg Charlie to come to England: "Oh honey pie, you are driving me frantic, sail across the Atlantic to be where you belong."

Charlie felt that the Beatles were beaming subliminal messages that, on a conscious level, were perhaps unknown even to the Fab Four themselves. During the Tate/LaBianca trial, Manson was quoted as saying: "I think it's a subconscious thing. I don't know whether they did it or not. But it's there. It's an association in the subconscious. This music is bringing on the revolution, the unorganized overthrow of the Establishment. The Beatles know in the sense that the subconscious knows."

According to Tex Watson and Paul Watkins, Manson's interpretation of *The White Album* was much more significant than Charlie was willing to later admit. It was their contention that *The White Album* was both a message to this "returned Jesus" (Charlie) to speak out, to call the chosen, and as a preparation for Helter Skelter. According to the Manson mythos, the Beatles' were setting the stage for Charlie's message, and Charlie himself was to give the world an album that would light the fuse the Beatles had prepared. This album would be message songs, with subtle symbols aimed at different parts of society involved in the changes that were coming. Charlie's album would contain the "plan" which the Beatles were asking him to reveal in the song "Revolution #1." In the song "I Will", the Beatles urge Manson to speak the word: "And when at last I find you, your song will fill the air, sing it loud so I can hear you, make it easy to be near you."

Following is a list of other songs from *The White Album* that Manson allegedly interpreted as direct messages from the fab four angels:

- "Happiness is a Warm Gun" which instructed the Family to arm themselves for the coming race war.

- "Piggies" was all about fat rich capitalists pigs and how they deserved a "damn good whacking", which is exactly what the blacks were going to give them. The verse about piggies eating bacon with forks and knives might have, in fact, been acted out by the murdering Mansonoids as a form of "Aesthetic Terrorism" ala Leno LaBianca with a fork stuck in his stomach. "Pig" was written at the Tate residence, and "Death to Pigs" was written at the LaBianca's home.

- "Rocky Raccoon" was another reference to blacks.

- "Helter Skelter" was a prophecy about Manson emerging from the bottomless pit'. "Healter Skelter" [sic] was written at the LaBianca's home.

Number nine, number nine, number nine...

Easily the most experimental piece on *The White Album* is John Lennon's mind-blowing cacophony, "Revolution #9", the apparent result of ingesting handfuls of LSD-25 tabs and spending long hours with scattered tape loops feeding them backward and forwards through reel to reel machines. "Revolution #9" took on great significance to Manson, who equated it with Revelation 9.

In his book *Big Secrets*, William Poundstone analyzed separately each overlaid track of "Revolution #9", both backward and forward, discovering several interesting sound bites, none of which constituted actual backward masking. These were, most likely, inadvertent accidents that found their way to vinyl by sheer dumb luck, when Lennon fed tape splices of archived BBC recordings into reel-to-reel machines. Because of this unorthodox recording process, many were led to believe, including Charlie, that hidden messages had been deliberately inserted as backward masked subliminals: a strange collage of taped sounds--warfare, church hymns, crying babies, football games, BBC announcers, and rock music--thrown together in overlapping anarchic patterns.

One example of backward masked subliminals is of a high strung voice screaming, "Let me out! Let me out!" Many took this as an allusion to Paul McCartney in his totaled Astin-Martin, screaming for help as he lay dying in the wreckage. This was a popular Beatle urban legend: that McCartney had died sometime prior to the *Sgt. Pepper* album, and an impostor, Billy Shears, had been brought in to take his place.

By far the most well-known and mind-blowing message to be found in "Revolution#9" is the "Number Nine-Turn Me On Dead Man" phonetic reversal, which Poundstone says is a quite common reversal, adding in his analysis that there was nothing special done in the recording process to have made this phenomenon occur. Anyone, Poundstone goes on to explain, who records their voice, saying, "Number Nine" and plays it backward will achieve the same effect: "Turn me on, dead man."

Like Manson, the number 9 held great significance in John Lennon's life. In numerology, 9 is the final number, the last single digit and highest counting number before starting over again; the beginning and the end. It was perhaps for these reasons that Lennon felt himself tuned into number 9, understanding the importance it played in his life.

Lennon's numerological odyssey began with his birth on October 9, 1940; his son Sean was also born on October 9. As a Liverpudian lad, Lennon grew up in England at 9 Newcastle Road. Brian Epstein discovered the Beatles on November 9, 1961. The Beatles played their first gig at the Cavern Club in '61. Nine years later--in 1970--they officially split up. The group rocketed to superstardom after appearing on the Ed Sullivan Show on February 9, 1964. Several of Lennon's tunes featured the number 9 theme, such as "Revolution #9" on *The White Album* and "Number 9 Dream" from *Walls and Bridges*. John married Yoko in '69. (He met her on November 9, 1966.) They moved from England to New York in '71, and lived there for nine years, until Lennon was shot to death outside the entrance of The Dakota on December 8, 1980. After receiving the fatal gunshots, Lennon was transported to Roosevelt Hospital on 9th Street, and was officially pronounced dead at 11:07 pm (1+1+7=9). In England, John's birthplace, it was already December 9.

The Dakota Building is located on West 72nd Street. (7+2=9) The Lennon's apartment number at The Dakota was 72. (Once again, 7+2=9.) Above Lennon's bed at the Dakota hung the number 9. Eerily enough, one of the apartment buildings Lennon purchased at The Dakota was used in the making of Roman Polanski's occult classic, *Rosemary's Baby*. According to author R. Gary Patterson, when Lennon discovered the *Rosemary's Baby* connection, he purportedly wrote "Helter Skelter" on the wall in the apartment, then moved a file cabinet in front of the wall to hide the words.

The Beatles' last album, *Abbey Road*, was recorded in 1969. In '69, Lennon officially changed his name from John Winston Lennon to John Ono Lennon, bragging that between John Ono Lennon and Yoko Ono Lennon there were nine O's. Lennon claimed to have seen a UFO while standing on the roof of The Dakota at 9 a.m. John and Yoko's Tarot card reader performed a pagan nuptial ceremony in '75 to celebrate their 6th wedding anniversary; the ceremony commenced at 9pm.

August 8th and 9th--when the Tate-LaBianca killings occurred--coincide with other significant dates in human history.

- On August 9, 1945, the atomic bomb was dropped on Nagasaki effectively drawing World War II to an Apocalyptic end.

- On August 8, 1907, famed cannibalistic serial killer Ed Gein--on whom Hitchcock's *Psycho* was loosely based--was born.

- On August 8, 1985, the LAPD first announced that the Night Stalker--a satanic serial killer--was haunting the city.

- On August 8, 1974, Richard Milhous Nixon became the first President in history to resign from office.

- On August 8th, 1969, Disneyland opened the doors to a new attraction, The Haunted Mansion. Later that night macabre history was made again on 10050 Cielo Drive when Sharon Tate and her house guests were murdered. The next evening, on August 9, the Mansonoids paid a visit to the LaBianca's house, formerly owned by Walt Disney.

Flowers and Blood

Out of the Summer of Love
Came the children of flowers and blood
With coffins in their eyes
Searching for the truth
In a graveyard full of lies.

Their messiah was their father and lover
Around the campfire he'd sing of love for brother
And of a bottomless pit below
A land of milk and honey
Far away from the evils of the world
The piggies and their money.

Tiny monsters made in some mad guru's mind
Bathing in a false light of love
That turns a wise man blind
Leading soon to darkness
Down a primrose path of blood
Lost in acid orgies, paranoia fueled by drugs.

And now the children come at you
With murder in their eyes
Revolution Number Nine is their lullaby
Dune buggies roarin' cross the desert, dust to dust
Dune buggies in decay, their ancient bodies rust.

The Summer of Love was a passing wave
Kent State and Altamont put it in a grave
The ghosts of '69 are with us to this day
Wrinkled and behind bars
Growing old and gray.

Twelve Spooky Fingers

I was deflating 1950's era gangsters with an invisible psychic force emanating from my fingertips until finally the bad guys lay flat on the ground like empty balloons. Thus I came to the sudden realization that I was dreaming.

With this realization, I could feel my control--just as I'd become aware of lucidity--slipping away. I caught a glimpse of my hands and remembered the Castaneda method my friend John Carter had once mentioned, the one where you look at your hands to preserve the state of lucid dreaming. John said that when he tried this himself, he saw ten to twenty fingers on each hand, then immediately awoke from the dream. When I looked at my hands in this manner I saw six spooky fingers that glowed with an iridescent sheen. Things were getting progressively weirder with the air around me now resembling a Van Gogh painting, as I then began to fade from this lucid state of "dreaming awake."

Upon waking a few scattered thoughts crossed my hazy mind. Was I in some way related to the race of creatures associated with the Alien Autopsy film? I chuckled inwardly at the premise, but took more seriously my following thoughts, which questioned the possibility of a psychic war taking place behind my closed eyelids within the realm of sleep. When I had gazed at my six-fingered hands I felt the presence in my dream of another psychic force intervening, just as I had awakened to the possibility of lucid dreaming.

The battle, it appears, is to keep us asleep, in the dark, unaware of the possibility of controlling our own realities, whether asleep *or* awake. I attempted, in the dream, to see my hands as they are, and was interrupted in this process by an intervening force, which added an extra digit on either hand as an attempt to wrestle away my "dream control." The actual battle in my dream was not with the deflated gangsters; they were just a convenient metaphor. The true battle exists with forces residing in the astral/dream plane, who tried to blow away my control--like I did re: the gangsters--with swirling Van Gogh winds that mesmerized my mind to the lucid possibilities of my own dream-plane dominion.

By what I gather from the dream journals of Jeff Lewis, he is likewise involved in a similar psychic battleground of the slumbering mind. His battle is one waged against the biblical gods of old who, Jeff contends, through the ages have maintained a stranglehold upon our collective dreams and visions, both asleep and awake, influencing history in the process. In some recent literature I received from Joseph Kerrick, he wrote in--what seemed to me--a similar vein in regards to a man "Seizing his autonomy back from the gods."

So, is this our great challenge as we plunge headfirst into the apocalyptic millennium? Is our only true means of salvation and surviving The Rapture by destroying the gods of yore and reclaiming the power that is rightfully ours? By rebuilding the Throne of God in Man's own graven image?

After all, it wasn't Eve's invitation that initiated Adam's naked fall from grace; it was the fear of unleashing his own untapped powers, when he tasted of the fruit plucked from The Tree of Knowledge.

Does this sound crazy?

Jeffery Lewis comments on "Twelve Spooky Fingers"

Dear Adam,

I think it appropriate I respond immediately to your letter, piece. Thanks for sending it, by the way.

Two nights ago I had a dream--vision in which a person with multiple fingers beyond 5 figured. I never got a precise count--but as many as 8 and up to five joints (pun) on some of them. I was engaged...rather reluctantly with this person in a form of "Olympic athletic" competition involving track and field events. It reminded me of the contest between "Pan" and "Ruffio" in *Hook*. Mostly I found it unimportant because not real.

In any event, the fellow I was contesting with had up to 8 fingers. Some of which resembled tree roots. I wondered has this person "uprooted" himself? Ever see Blake's pictures of Tree people in Hell? So, maybe I was seeing your lucidity work--you uprooting yourself from the unconscious slave work (in Egypt, sold into slavery--Joseph) that is required of all dreamers to support The Kingdom, Pharaoh?

Seems a good guess. If so, keep it up. I find "lucidity" less important than an ability to re-enter dream space consciously, with complete consciousness.

The Van Gogh landscape is an important element and would probably be "Hell." The elements of mental illness, madness there--yes? "Inspiration."

I'm delighted you're aware of my work. Keep up a correspondence if you wish.

Best,
Jeff Lewis

P.S. R.A. Lafferty wrote stories featuring multiple fingers. It was an indication of some form of talent.

The Word

God came to me, and said,
"I, your lord God, am not real,
forget me, go on living.
There's so little time to do,
don't waste your time in
thoughts of me.
I am untouchable, unattainable
in this revolving world of flesh.
I come to you only when you
come to yourself.
Hold your heart in your hands
and you will hold a part of me,
or a measure of yourself
reflecting my image."

"You are a child no longer.
You need no father
with invisible hands to guide you.
If you do not scale the mountains yourself,
how will you ever lose your fear of heights?
If you do not plunge into the ocean,
how will you ever learn to swim?"

God said, "Kill me,
so that you may learn to live."

An Interpretation of Kubrick's *Eyes Wide Shut*

In Stanley Kubrick's final film, *Eyes Wide Shut*, there are numerous veiled allusions to the CIA's MK-ULTRA mind control experiments and Monarch sex slave programming. According to victims of Monarch abuse, their ranks number literally in thousands, and it has been alleged that these very same victims have been used extensively as sex slaves, drug mules and assassins. According to varied sources, Monarch programming begins at birth, and is carried out through the lives of its victims, as they are used by intelligence agencies and secret societies like pawns on a gameboard, until--in many instances--they have outlived their usefulness, and are terminally "discarded". According to Per Sewen of Illuminati News, he viewed *Eyes Wide Shut* with a woman who had been "subjected to Satanic Ritual Abuse (SRA) by the Illuminati and she found it very, very accurate. None of us had any idea what the movie was about, so it was a shock for both of us, especially as these kinds of movies can be very triggering for victims of SRA. And it was. This girl didn't feel well afterwards..."

Associating the "Bavarian Illuminati"--as it was originally identified--with the ominous spectre of mind control is a controversial subject, as the presumed current day existence of this secret order is not an easy thing to document, although fringe Christians and right wing extremists would have us believe that The Illuminati has been behind nearly every crucial development in the history of mankind over the past few hundred years; from the French and American Revolutions to the forthcoming New World Order/One World Government takeover, not to mention the Kennedy Assassination and water fluoridation. In response, I would not totally dispute this proposition, nor do I wholeheartedly endorse it, preferring instead to straddle the fence between shadow and light, at the crossroads where fact and fancy meet. It is at this meeting point where we are briefly allowed a glimpse of the truth, while at the same time the edges of the picture blur, leaving us once again in a quandary. (Or a Philip K. Dick novel...)

According to certain legends, the Illuminati was purged in 1785 by the Bavarian Government on the grounds that it had attempted to overthrow the European ruling class. Other legends suggest that the Illuminati were merely driven underground at this juncture, all the while continuing their multifarious activities under a maze of guises-- including such current incarnations as the Bilderbergers, The United Nations and the Council of Foreign Relations--and exist unto this day, pulling the levers behind the scenes of world events, albeit hidden behind a cloak of subterfuge and secrecy. Other researchers contend that the Illuminati is simply a subdivision of Freemasonry, this due to the fact that the original Order of the Illuminati was formed within Masonic Lodges in Germany, by one Adam Weishaupt in 1776. According to Robert Anton Wilson, who has spent many years attempting to unravel this mystery: "Since Masonry itself is a secret society, the Illuminati was a secret society within a secret society, a mystery inside a mystery, so to say." Arcane history lesson aside, I will henceforth use the term "Illuminati" rather liberally throughout this tract, as an easy catchall which captures under its umbrella a wide-ranging hierarchy of hidden powers; a combination of intelligence agencies and secret societies creating an Orwellian nightmare under the guise of a New World Utopia. Bear in mind that the secret society in *Eyes Wide Shut* are never identified as the "Illuminati". Since this is "an interpretation", I have freely chosen to exercise my poetic license, using "Illuminati" as a simple literary device, although nothing is ever quite as simple as we would like it to be. Once again, we're speaking here of the shadow realms, like those hinted at in *Eyes Wide Shut*, where nothing is ever for certain, nor can anything be taken for granted.

Early on in *Eyes Wide Shut*--while at a lavish party hosted by a rich bigwig named Ziegler (played by Sydney Pollack)--Tom Cruise's character, Dr. Bill, is seduced by two beautiful "models" who take him by either arm, leading him toward an apparent menage a trois. When Dr. Bill asks where exactly they're taking him, the two lovelies reply: "Where the rainbow ends." When taken into context with what transpires later in *Eyes Wide Shut*, this snatch of dialog appears to be an allusion to Monarch programming, as *The Wizard of Oz* has been long acknowledged by Monarch insiders as a common programming matrix, which uses Wizard of Oz themes and imagery as a tool to program minds. (It has been rumored that Judy Garland herself was the subject of just this sort of Monarch-styled mind control.)

Later, Dr. Bill rents a cloak and mask from "Rainbow Costumes", which just happens to be located above another shop called "Under The Rainbow". In the first scene at the costume shop, the owner catches his underage daughter in a state of undress with two apparent drag queens, and understandably becomes quite upset. In a later scene, the shop owner does an about-face and appears not only to be pimping out his nubile daughter to these very same drag queens, but tries to interest Dr. Bill in her pert young bod, as well. This is all very telling, as most Wizard of Oz programming I've heard about allegedly deals with the programming of boys and girl--at a very early age--in their roles as Monarch slaves, through sexual molestation and other related trauma such as SRA, as part of a pact between the parents of the abused children and their Monarch "handlers". (In many instances--it has been alleged--the parent will also perform the role of "handler". The "handler, in essence, is the "programmer", as well as a sort of go-between with the higher ups in the Monarch organization.) Whatever the case, something drastically "transformed" the costume shop owner's way of thinking, between the first and the second scenes, in a space of less than 24 hours. The inference here is that the Illuminati-styled cult that Dr. Bill stumbles upon is somehow responsible for this "trance-formation" of father to pimp and daughter to prostitute. This is part of the symbolism of Monarch, one of transformation, of caterpillar into butterfly; free-will into mental slavery. The term Monarch is deceptive in this sense, due to its identification with the Monarch butterfly, a creature of transformational beauty. This appears to be part of the deception of this programming; to delude its victims into believing they've been transformed into something magical, and full of wonder. *Follow the yellow brick road.*

Although the "trance-formation" of the shop owner's daughter seems unrelated to later events that occur in the film, somehow these two seemingly anecdotal characters--the shop owner and his daughter--have been affected by Dr. Bill's Illuminati-sex-ritual experience. The implication here is that anyone who comes within the span of Dr. Bill is, by association, caught up in a similar web of intrigue, often resulting in dire consequences.

Another MK-ULTRA/Monarch allusion is the reference to the "models" who seduce Dr. Bill at Ziegler's party, which I associate with what is known in the annals of MK-ULTRA lore as "Presidential models". "Presidential models" were/are allegedly used by big time entertainers and politicians as sexual playthings; mind controlled puppets programmed to perform assorted perverse acts at the bidding of their manipulative "handlers". Allegedly, Marilyn Monroe was the first Monarch sex slave who achieved "celebrity" status. For those unfamiliar with the term "Presidential model", I'll refer them to *The Control of Candy Jones* by Donald Bain and Long John Nebel. As the story goes, Long John Nebel--a New York radio personality in the 50's-70's--discovered (via hypnosis) that his wife, Candy Jones, was a victim of just this sort of mind control project, one of the many MK-ULTRA mind slaves, programmed by CIA "spychiatrists" and used by high mucky muck dignitaries to perform their perverse sexual whims, among other assorted duties such as being used as drug mules and message couriers for this vast network of corrupt power brokers. More has come to light in this regard in recent years by way of similar allegations disbursed widely across the Internet, as well as such highly controversial books as *Trance Formation In America* by Mark Phillips and Kathy O'Brien, wherein Ms. O'Brien relates her own troubling tales of MK-ULTRA and Monarch abuse. Once again, the tricky part is trying to untangle this web of fact vs. fiction, for a great measure of the Monarch mythos is the obvious result of contaminated stories, planted as a means of discrediting the victims. For example: the current trend of shape-shifting Reptilian extraterrestrials who have entered into the mind control lexicon of late, such as one purported Monarch victim has described ex-President George Bush, among a group of other world leaders, who double as alien lizards and smack-shooting Satanists. As the late Jim Keith noted in his final book, *Mass Control*: "By injecting outlandish details into these stories, by linking intelligence agency mind control with extraterrestrial aliens and such, a pallor of doubt is cast upon real cases of abuse. This is the activity of 'scrambling' that Katherine Sullivan and others talk about. It is also true that traumatic abuse and conditioning confuses and disorients the victim, causing cross-referencing of mental information, and potentially adding to the nightmarish quality of many reports of this sort."

Before the two "models" are able to lead Dr. Bill on a journey to "Where the rainbow ends", he is called to the aid of his host, Mr. Ziegler, who is upstairs, trying to revive a naked beauty O.D.-ing in his bathroom. Dr. Bill helps Ziegler revive the sultry junkie from her self-induced speedball funk. As fickle fate would have it, this naked beauty later resurfaces in the film as Dr. Bill's savoir, and is--in my estimation--another of the many Monarch sex slaves who appear throughout the story. From there the film progresses into the previously alluded meeting of a secret order akin to the Illuminati, of which Dr. Bill inadvertently gains knowledge of, and sneaks into, undercover of mask and cloak--as all the other participants are likewise bedecked--in what he soon realizes is some sort of Satanic/Freemasonic sex magick rite featuring a whole host of naked hotties engaged in steamy sex scenes right out of an Aleister Crowley freak-out. When it's discovered by this Illuminati-like group that they have a spy in their fold in the form of Dr. Bill, Cruise's character is taken before the High Priest and his mask ceremoniously removed. Just when it looks like curtains for Dr. Bill, a well-proportioned lady--adorned only in mask and high-heeled shoes--steps before the assembly and offers herself up in sacrifice in exchange for Dr. Bill's life. As it turns out, this is the same woman, Mandy, that Dr. Bill rescued earlier from an overdose. (Drug addiction is a common modus operandi in the control of Monarch sex slaves.) Long story short, Mandy is apparently sacrificed, although the next day newspaper reports characterize her passing as an apparent O.D. The deeper meaning here is that all Monarch sex slaves are expendable if they cross the line, and many of these victims reportedly have been discarded in just such a manner after they become a certain age and are no longer desirable as prostitute/sex slaves, or if they in someway break free of their programming and are considered a risk.

During his dark night of the soul, Dr. Bill travels through the seamy underworld of his disturbed psyche, searching for sexual release, haunted by some insatiable hunger driving him toward unknown ends, along the way encountering a woman he hardly knows, who swears she's madly in love with him. Add to this collection an HIV positive prostitute, as well as the daughter of the aforementioned costume shop owner--who's apparently being pimped out by her papa--and what we have is a trinity of lost souls, caught up in the grinding wheels of a powerful machine that eats people up, then spits them out in tiny, fragmented pieces. Monarch programming would explain the actions of all three: the irrational love of the woman Dr. Bill hardly knows is characteristic of a mind controlled slave programmed to love someone without truly understanding the reasons why; likewise the prostituted daughter, a common thread of Monarch programming where parents sell their children into sexual bondage and generational molestation as part of a deal made with the "Illuminati". And lastly, the common prostitute, there to do the bidding of the men who manipulate her by way of either money, drugs or violence. All of these woman could easily be Monarch victims, and even if they aren't, each is a prisoner of a system of control prevalent in our society; a system which exists on many levels, and in all strata, both seen and unseen. *Eyes Wide Shut* is a glimpse into these dark, shadow realms.

Many people unfamiliar with the subtleties of mind control will be utterly perplexed with the allegorical symbolism in *Eyes Wide Shut*. The characters, for the most part, appear either as detached spectators (i.e. hypnotized subjects) or obsessed sex fiends forever in search of a carnal fix. Unlike other Kubrick films--where the characters, in most cases, are more well-developed, complex characterizations--those in *Eyes Wide Shut* seem mere cardboard cutouts, which I think is the desired effect Kubrick was striving for. Victims of mind control are just these sorts of automatons, stumbling through life blind to the true significance of their actions, lost in the fog of their work-a-day world, mere stringed puppets who believe they control their own destinies. The reason there appears to be no true depth to the characters in *Eyes Wide Shut* is that their inner depth has been buried beneath layers of mind control. What I believe Kubrick was hinting at, in *Eyes Wide Shut*, is that we are all mind controlled in one sense or another, sleep walking through our lives with "eyes wide shut"; "Manchurian Candidates" who kill without understanding the true motivations behind their acts. Even Nichole Kidman's character, Alice, who appears to be complicated, and seemingly multifaceted--a lady of many moods--is in reality a simple caricature who wears many involuntary masks, shedding one for no apparent rhyme or reason, and then donning another for equally vague motivations, unknown even to herself. Each mask is merely a new and different role; each mask an alter ego, with no true relation to the core personality. Ala Gurdjieff, she is a mere meat machine, sleep-walking through her life.

The choice of Cruise and Kidman in these roles is, to say the least, curious. Their emotional depth as actors--throughout their respective careers--has always appeared suspect, in my opinion. I sincerely doubt that either of them were actually perceptive enough to grasp what Kubrick was getting at with this film, which is perhaps just the sort of emotional content--or lack thereof--that the director was looking for from his characters. *Eyes wide shut*. This emotional complacency, for want of a better term, seems to go hand in hand with the duos involvement in Scientology, in whose members I have always perceived a certain lack of self-awareness. Call it brainwashing, or whatever you wish, this is simply a visceral observation on my part, and should not be construed as a total condemnation of Scientology. In all fairness, the Church of Scientology has long been outspoken about the abuses of MK-ULTRA, as documented often in the pages of their magazine *Freedom*, not to mention L. Ron Hubbard himself, who during his later years was a vocal critic of the CIA and their involvement in MK-ULTRA shenanigans.

For those unfamiliar with the subtle spectre of secret societies and their peculiar practices, there will be obvious confusion as to why Dr. Bill immediately becomes a marked man just because he happened upon some seemingly harmless kinky scene with a bunch of guys and gals wearing masks, chanting meaningless mumbo-jumbo and humping one another like a pack of dogs in heat; a provocative spectacle, indeed, but certainly not enough to mark a man for death, one would presume. Well, the deeper implication here is that Dr. Bill has become not only an unwitting witness to a sex orgy of Hell Fire Club-like proportions, but more importantly, a witness to Monarch sex programming, and ostensibly a potential threat to National Security if he were to reveal these dire, dreaded secrets, that even he himself doesn't quite know what to make of.

After his close call with these evil Illuminati-type characters, the plot thickens ever more as Dr. Bill is pursued by his own inner sexual demons--through one sordid scene after another--finally discovering that his wife, Alice, has had a "dream" where she was a participant in a similar Illuminati-styled sex orgy. These memories come to Alice during a "dream", which in reality appears to be a repressed memory; a "dream" featuring a "Naval Officer" with a penetrating stare, that Alice once saw while on vacation years earlier; a "Naval Officer" who seemingly hypnotized her for a brief instant, as they passed each other in a hotel lobby one day, and since then she had been haunted by the memory of his penetrating stare, so much so that she can't get it out of her mind. Anyway, it is this "Naval Officer" who enters Alice's dream like some sort of MK-Incubus, and--after having his way with her-- initiates Alice into this aforementioned Illuminati-type sex orgy- nightmare, where she gives herself up to all takers, albeit within a supposed dream-state. Here, once again, the student of Monarch lore must exercise their poetic license, connecting the dots and placing into context this veiled allusion to the mysterious "Naval Officer" who possessed Alice's thoughts--in both the sleeping and waking worlds-- and from there draw a parallel between the "Naval Officer" to Naval Intelligence, a branch of the Armed Forces that has long been an active participant in MK-ULTRA operations. The Naval Officer in this instance is merely symbolic of a larger hierarchy of mass mind control. On another note, a branch of Scientology--known as "Sea-Orgs"--uses naval-type uniforms in their organization, which is another chilling parallel when taken into context with Cruise and Kidman's involvement in the church. Perhaps I'm way off course here, but I feel this "coincidence" bears mentioning.

At the end of *Eyes Wide Shut*--as the credits rolled by--my central thought was: "Who the hell wrote this?" I don't recall the author's name now, but the credits said the screenplay was based on a book called *Trauma-ville*, which I indeed found to be a troubling title, as the main tool used in MK-ULTRA/Monarch mind control is what is known as "trauma based programming". According to alleged victims of this type of abuse, various types of trauma--both physical and psychological--are used to create disassociated states known as "alters", or multiple personalities. Alters are a way of splitting off the victim from their core personality, and as a means of self-defense the victims themselves use to escape from the induced trauma, by adopting another personality, or "alter"-ego who is completely unaware of the trauma experienced by the core personality. It is a psychological means of putting on a mask to hide from the awful truth of this type of abuse, and at the same time a calculated result of "trauma based programming". This explains the significance of the masks that are used in the film during the big sex orgy scene, as the Monarch victims have switched to their sex slave personalities, adopting one of their many programmed "alters". Through "trauma based programming" a whole host of alters can be purportedly created and induced; alters unknown to the core personality, such as the aforementioned sex slave personality, or "Manchurian Candidate"-type assassins like a Sirhan Sirhan, who commit murder while in an "alter"-ed state of mind, and then afterwards possess no memory of the actual event which transpired.

Likewise, *Eyes Wide Shut* is a curious title for this film, for what it suggests is that information is being processed, while simultaneously the conscious mind is deep asleep, totally unaware, subliminally filing this information into the subconscious where it can be used later to nefarious ends by the handlers of these mind controlled victims. This is similar to what conspiracy researcher Michael Anthony Hoffman II calls the "Revelation of the Method" and "The Making Manifest Of All That Is Hidden", which is the subtle processing of humankind using these insidious tools of trance-formation, whether done individually or on a wide-scale level through television, mass media, and the movies. It is for this reason--some have hinted--that Kubrick met his fate just prior to the completion of *Eyes Wide Shut*: for ostensibly spilling the beans of what goes on behind the scenes in regards to secret societies and intelligence agencies who use mind control to program the masses. In this context, Kubrick may have been playing a part in ushering in the New World Order of The Illuminati, but to his own misfortune revealed "too much, too soon", thus a possible reason for his sudden passing. In Hoffman's *Secret Societies and Psychological Warfare*, he states that "...the Revelation of the Method has as its chief component, a clown-like, grinning mockery of the victim(s) as a show of power and macabre arrogance. When this is performed in a veiled manner accompanied by certain occult sign and symbolical words and elicits no meaningful response of opposition or resistance from the target(s), it is one of the most efficacious techniques of psychological warfare and mind-rape..."

One of the most memorable scenes from *Eyes Wide Shut* is when Cruise and Kidman are embracing in front of a mirror, a prelude to sex.

According to Monarch researchers Cisco Wheeler and Fritz Springmeier: "...in programming Monarch slaves, mirrors are used a great deal. Within the Monarch slave's mind, countless mirror images are made. The slave sees thousands of mirrors everywhere in their mind. Because Marilyn (Monroe) was so stripped of any personal identity, she decorated her house as her mind looked on the inside--full of mirrors. Although other Monarchs may have some desires to decorate with mirrors, Marilyn is the most extreme case I know of filling one's house full of mirrors..."

In this mirror scene--as Dr. Bill and Alice are engaged in an erotic embrace--Alice twice gazes into the mirror, and her reflection could be interpreted as an expression of either guilt or confusion. In Monarch programming, mirrors have been reportedly employed as a means of triggering alters and causing disassociation, which is my interpretation of this scene: Alice is engaged in what is known in Monarch programming as "switching." The supposition of Alice as mind control victim explains much of what unfolds throughout the course of the film, as her character is one possessing a great many contradictions, and inexplicable moods. At Ziegler's party--while dancing with a rich foreign aristocrat--Alice adopts the persona of an intoxicated, flighty airhead. At other times throughout the film she is smart and sophisticated, then alternately cold and cruel; at other times a caring mother, and a devoted wife. After a few hits off a joint, Alice goes on a tirade where she becomes both jealous and judgmental of her husband, initiating a heated argument. It is telling that after a toke or two of the killer weed, Alice's mood shifts so precipitously, as drugs are another well-established tool used in Monarch programming for triggering "alters". What I'm suggesting here is that Alice is just that, a victim of Monarch programming. When--toward the end of the film--Dr. Bill's missing mask is discovered upon a pillow next to his sleeping wife, a message has been delivered, clear and simple, that the same Illuminati mind controllers hounding Dr. Bill have all along had access to his wife, even while she sleeps, deep in the shadowy recesses of her unconscious mind. Whether their eyes are wide open or shut, there can be no escape.

MACK WHITE

O f the various cottage industries that have emerged from the field of conspiracy theory, the Montauk Project is easily one of the most bizarre, its mythology a veritable smorgasbord of "comic book metaphysics", as Disinformation's Richard Metzger has so aptly termed it.

Time travel, mind control, quantum physics, weather modification, teleportation, suppressed technologies, and grey alien hijinks merely scratch the surreal surface behind the many mind-blowing psychodramas detailed in the numerous books authored by the Montauk fraternity, such as *The Montauk Project: Experiments in Time, Montauk Revisited: Adventures in Synchronicity*, and *The Black Sun: Montauk's Nazi-Tibetan Connection*.

To the casual observer, the Montauk Project appears to be a hodge-podge of many diverse disciplines, much of which would be considered by the mainstream as "crank science." Take a little Wilhelm Reich, sprinkle it with Nichola Tesla, then add a dose of Aleister Crowley, and what you end up with is one magnificent mindfuck that goes off on so many tangents and arcane avenues that the mind boggles, either discounting this entire sordid tale, or conversely becoming so caught up and confused in this cosmic conundrum that the Montauk mythos becomes the focal point in their lives.

As legend has it, this whole weird tale began towards the end of World War II, an alleged result of the U.S. Government's top-secret Rainbow Project. According to varied sources, the initial goal of The Rainbow Project was to make a ship--specifically the *USS Eldridge*-- undetectable by radar. Such endeavors as The Rainbow Project were a precursor to future stealth fighter craft technology, or in the parlance of *Star Trek*, a "cloaking device." Although the experiment was allegedly successful in causing the Eldridge to disappear from the Philadelphia Naval Yard, it also had some bizarre side effects that took the project out of the realms of hard science and tossed it haphazardly into a raging sea of high weirdness. For you see, not only was the ship made invisible, but it also produced an unexpected consequence, in that it teleported the Eldridge and its crew a hundred miles away to Norfolk, Virginia, where it reappeared. It was then transported back again to the Philly Naval Yard where one crewmember was terminally planted into the bulkhead of the ship.

Those who survived the ordeal entered into a state of madness and terror, totally freaked-out by the events that had occurred. The Rainbow

Project--after its somewhat successful and equally ill-fated physical vanishing of the USS Eldridge--continued on after the 1940's, conducting covert experiments under the shadowy umbrella of U.S. Government Black Ops. This all presumably culminated in 1983 at a decommissioned Air Force station at Montauk Point when a hole was literally ripped through the space-time continuum. The end result of this Rainbow/Montauk technology was the creation of an alternate reality vortex. The Montauk Project is also referred to as The Phoenix Project, but to avoid any further confusion we'll refer to it from this point forward exclusively as the Montauk Project.

The Rainbow Project--which in recent times has become more popularly known as The Philadelphia Experiment--has been the subject of both a book and movie of the same name. *The Philadelphia Experiment: Project Invisibility* was co-authored by Charles Berlitz and William "Bill" Moore, a somewhat curious figure in the annals of UFO research. Long story short, Moore was intimately involved in the fabled Paul Bennewitz affair, and has been dubbed by many in Ufology as a disinformation agent, not only in regards to the aforementioned case concerning Paul Bennewitz and the Dulce underground base, but as well for his role in "uncovering" the infamous MJ-12 documents. For those unfamiliar with these respective cases, a simple web search on either Paul Bennewitz or MJ-12 will no doubt turn up a wealth of information--or disinformation, as the case may be. Such as it is, Mr. Moore's research into these areas should at least be taken with a grain of salt. It's the present author's opinion that disinformation scams (such as Alternative 3, MJ-12, etc.) have, more likely than not, been used to discredit serious research into such topics as mind control, hidden technologies, UFO's and covert Black Ops. What I'm suggesting is that there may be a certain amount of truth surrounding the Montauk case, but a means of obscuring and distorting truth can sometimes be accomplished by releasing spurious stories that do indeed contain within them a measure of truth, but are also so thoroughly littered with red herrings that sincere researchers are diverted off course, and the theory itself becomes so muddied with misinformation that it's hard to take it seriously at all, as such seems to be the case in regards to much of the Project Montauk mythos.

In regards to the producer of *The Philadelphia Experiment* movie, an even greater curiosity abounds. According to the official scribe for the Montauk investigation, Peter Moon, the actor Mark Hamill--who played Luke Skywalker in the *Star Wars Trilogy*--is the actual producer of the film, though he chooses to keep this fact hidden from the public.

It has been hinted at by Peter Moon that a gentleman named Mark Knight (aka Mark Hamill) was a childhood friend of Montauk experiencer Preston Nichols, and that Hamill was instrumental in securing work for Nichols as a sound engineer on *The Empire Strikes Back*. It should also be noted that Hamill's father was an officer with Naval Intelligence, an agency long rumored to be mired in mind control conspiracies and assorted covert operations, one of which was, allegedly, the Montauk Project. Furthermore, Moon contends that Mark Hamill worked at Montauk during its halcyon days of time travel shenanigans and mind control meddlings. Curiouser and curiouser...

For the average Jane and Joe--whose ideas about alternate dimensions come directly from the rental of an occasional sci-fi flick-- The Philadelphia Experiment remains naught but a fictional flight of fancy, although researchers--many of them Montauk alumni--claim to have in their possession actual documents verifying the existence of the project! In fact, on the covers of many a Montauk book, it's boldly advertised that the book series, "Goes beyond science fiction." In other words, beyond the point of believability. What I do find refreshing, though, is that the likes of Preston Nichols, Al Bielek, et al., flatly state that they're not trying to prove anything in particular, but are simply presenting the facts as they perceive them, and it's up to the rest of us to derive some meaning from all this Montaukian madness. (Or write it all off as mere delusion--or out and out disinformation.) In a sense, this is the same ontological approach of such pioneers of quantum physics and consciousness exploration as Robert Anton Wilson, who adopt a philosophy of perceiving reality as an ever-changing façade which we as humans must interpret, then translate to fit into our own particular reality tunnels or world views. Or failing that, take the approach that all life is indeed Maya, much like a Philip K. Dick novel where you never know from one instant to the next if the ground is going to fall out from under your feet. For those who have extensively studied the occult and/or taken trips down psychedelic highways and byways, it quickly becomes evident that physical reality is merely one way to skin an ontological cat, so to simply rule out the seemingly far-out assertions of Al Bielek and Preston Nichols is a little short sighted in this author's opinion, though on the same token I'd be leery of buying a used time machine from either one of these blokes.

Preston Nichols--one of the key players in the Montauk story--was an apparent unwitting participant in the project, who years after the fact finally discovered his actual involvement in matters Montaukian. Since that time he has been sharing his strange story through lectures, books and videos. For those unfamiliar with the man, Nichols cuts a quite memorable swath. One part Jabba the Hutt and the other part some sort of psychic superhero/electronic genius with an unnatural fondness for virile young men.

Nichols--a veritable high-tech wizard--has his own version of the Mystery Machine in the form of a retired and renovated school bus, or as he calls it, his "Montauk Investigation vehicle." Nichol's bus is filled with all sorts of gadgets and gizmos he allegedly salvaged from the secret Montauk site. Not only has Nichols been instrumental in bringing the Montauk Project story to a mass audience, but he has also (allegedly) played a pivotal role in deprogramming several Montaukian mind controlled subjects, more commonly known as the Montauk Boys, a slew of young men with Aryan characteristics, who had been covertly recruited into the Montauk mind control project. The ulterior motive behind this phase of the project was to create a blond-haired, blue-eyed bloodline of future rulers of the earth, thus bringing forth The New World Order.

During their original programming, the Montauk Boys were entranced via some sort of MK-ULTRA/psychosexual programming. For those unfamiliar with MK-ULTRA, it was a CIA covert mind control project started in 1953 under a program exempt from congressional oversight. MK-ULTRA agents and "spychiatrists" tested radiation, electric shock, microwaves, and electrode implants on unwitting subjects. Other intelligence agencies--such as the NSA and Naval Intelligence--were also involved in this covert experimentation, and it's quite likely that the Montauk Project was a continuation of same. It has also been documented that Nazi doctors--covertly imported into the US after World War II--were instrumental in the early years of the MK-ULTRA project, as much of the early research into mind control was conducted on concentration camp victims by the likes of Joseph Mengele, and other notorious Nazi doctors. Apparently, this legacy was continued in Montauk's underground facility.

Back in the 1970's--according to Peter Moon--the Montauk group became interested in programming children. The story gets even wackier when grey aliens become part of the lore, reportedly kidnapping around fifty children and delivering them to Montauk for these experiments.

In regards to Preston Nichol's deprogramming of the Montauk Boys, this was supposedly accomplished by masturbating these young men in concert with radionics. The method behind this madness-- according to Preston Nichols and associates--suggests that in order to deprogram the Montauk Boys, they first had to be taken into the same trance state in which they were originally programmed. Once there,

114

Nichols would then be able to undo the previous programming by using similar mind control tactics, which included tantric massage, and certain other unspecified "Reichian Techniques". Some would suggest that all of this Montaukian madness is simply a cover on the part of Preston Nichols for homoerotic perversions, though whether or not he was actually getting his jollies jerking off the Montauk Boys is purely a matter of speculation. Admittedly, I'm not all too familiar with Reichian Therapy, except that it apparently falls in line with Dr. Wilhelm Reich's overall worldview that the basic fundamental energy pumping life into the cosmos is the sex drive, and that this energy is defined in Reichian terms as "Orgone Energy". Part of Reich's therapy (if I'm not mistaken) had to do with removing the layers of psychic armoring that turns large segments of humankind into a bunch of repressed and uptight, sexually dysfunctional tight-asses. It must be understood that the intent of Reich's various therapies was not so much to control minds, as it was to set them free, but apparently Montaukian mind controllers took certain elements of these Reichian therapies and used them in a manner Reich had not originally intended.

For those not in the know, Wilhelm Reich was a one time student of Sigmund Freud, who went on to establish himself in the fields of psychology, science and alternative heath. Father of the "Orgone Box", Reich was later persecuted by the FDA on the pretext of being some sort of sexually deviant quack. Many of his published materials were subsequently burned via Gestapo-like tactics by FDA officials, and because of his controversial research, Reich was unjustly imprisoned. A common perception of Reich supporters is that he was railroaded into prison as a means the government used to suppress his alternative health cures and controversial research into such subjects as UFO's. Shortly after his imprisonment in the late 50's, Reich died of a heart attack, although he was not known previously to have had any heart problems. Some subscribe his premature death to a conspiracy. If such was the case, it evidently succeeded.

In regards to UFO's, Reich had some rather odd ideas, at least by conventional standards. His perspective was that UFO's were not so much actual nuts and bolts craft, as they were some sort of spectral space critters; interdimensional amoeba undulating throughout the known universe for unknown reasons. And if I haven't already cluttered your heads up enough with this deluge of diverse and possibly delusional info, Reich was also of the opinion that UFO's were powered by Orgone Energy, the aforementioned fundamental cosmic power source of the Universe. Seems that these Reichian perceived UFO-nauts had somehow tapped into the Orgone Energy grid of Earth, sucked up vast quantities of said substance, then spat out a form of exhaust that Reich referred to as Deadly Orgone (DOR).

DOR--Reich contended--was quickly destroying the environment. In response, Reich developed what came to be known in the annals of fringe science as the "Cloudbuster", which was basically a space gun that could be aimed directly at UFO's and cause them to disappear. The Cloudbuster also had the power to purportedly seed clouds with rain. Many thought Reich completely off his rocker in regards to his UFO theories, although the U.S. Air Force was quite interested in his research. As those who get deep into the Montauk story know, Reich is another famous name that comes up often in these discussions, as it appears his research is quite instrumental to the unfolding Montauk mythos.

Perhaps the most important piece of apparatus in this whole jumbled mess was the legendary Montauk Chair upon which Duncan Cameron (a psychic superstar in Project Montauk lore) sat and radiated his paranormal powers with the intent of creating artificial reality vortexes. The ultimate purpose of these experiments was to not only alter physical reality, but to alter as well the mental landscape of humankind.

The Montauk Chair itself--so states Preston Nichols--was developed in the 1950's with "sensor technology" that could display a person's thoughts, and was in essence a mind-reading machine. This device operated on the principle of tuning into the electromagnetic fields of human beings and translating their ethereal or Orgone Energy into a tangible form, ala thought-into-matter. This is where Duncan Cameron would sit in the Montauk Chair, his head blazing like a psychic furnace, and paint a mental landscape of the gods. It was in this regard that Duncan himself, it has been said, became likened unto a god. To make the legend even more abstruse, Montauk propagandists claim that beings from the Sirius star system are also tangled up in this convoluted tale. Apparently, the Sirians provided the basic design for the Montauk Chair, and then Montauk scientists took those original blueprints and developed it. The "Montauk Chair", in turn, was hooked into a complex grid of computers and amplifiers.

Eventually the Montauk Chair (which, in appearance, was not unlike a Lay- z- Boy lounger) was fine-tuned to the point where a person could visualize something and a 3D image of those thought-forms would appear on a computer monitor, and then could be printed out. But it's only when Duncan Cameron came into the picture that things really started getting out of hand.

In a deep psychic trance state, Cameron, at one point, was able to visualize a solid object and actually make it appear from out of nowhere. This was accomplished via an amplifier that would transmit a matrix, and then build up enough power to materialize whatever Cameron mentally cooked up, under the direction of his Montauk handlers. As indicated, Cameron took part in these experiments in an altered state of consciousness. In this regard, agents of the CIA and/or NSA--under the auspices of MK-ULTRA funded experiments--had given Cameron special training, according to Montauk legend. The emphasis of this programming focused on diverting the mind through sexual bliss. It was then that the "primitive mind" would surface, as the individual--in this case, Duncan Cameron--would be transferred into an orgasmic trance-state. His primitive mind--now at the disposal of nefarious Montauk operatives--would then become extremely suggestible, and therefore controllable.

In time--through the use of the Montauk Chair--it was discovered that Cameron had the power to bend time, thus creating vortexes, or time portals, not unlike the concept from the old TV series, *Time Tunnel*. In fact, those who have actually traveled through this time portal have described it like a spiral, such as that depicted in the aforementioned television series. Anyway, when Cameron would envision certain alternate realities in past and future time, the vortex could then be copied to the hard drive of Montauk computers. These experiments eventually led to a project with the express purpose of opening a time door to the USS Eldridge in 1943. All of this high-tech time travel tinkering is what allegedly sucked such players as Duncan Cameron and Al Bielek into the Montauk vortex. Bielek, for instance-- in another incarnation as Duncan Cameron's brother, Edward--was a member of the crew on board the USS Eldridge, and because of his alleged involvement with the Montauk Project has been jettisoned back and forth in time repeatedly, in the process leaving one body behind and assuming another.

Montauk Project participants (one of whom was Preston Nichols, although Nichols himself wasn't aware of this until after the fact because he'd been mind-controlled in such a Montaukian manner that he was actually living on two separate time tracks!) were given the directive on August 5th, 1983 to turn on the transmitter at Montauk and let run it non-stop. At first, nothing out of the ordinary happened. Then, on August 12th, the equipment apparently dropped into synch with the USS Eldridge, which suddenly appeared on the other end of the time portal. It was at this juncture that the Duncan Cameron from 1943 (who was an earlier incarnation of the present day Duncan Cameron)

117

appeared in the time portal along with his brother, who in present day earth is non-other than Al Bielek. (Confused yet???) It seems that the past tense Duncan and Edward had tried to sabotage the Philadelphia Experiment by shutting down the equipment aboard the Eldridge, but found this to be an impossible task as it was all linked through time to the generator at Montauk. (Don't ask me to explain that one, either!) Determining that it was unsafe to remain aboard the ship, they decided to jump overboard to free themselves from the electromagnetic field surrounding it. Upon so doing, the Brother's Cameron were pulled through a time tunnel and on to dry ground, materializing at Montauk on August 12th, 1983! If you've been able to follow this thread thus far, I applaud you, as this whole story is naught but an endless maze that transports us back and forth through time, out of one crazy portal and into another.

When the Cameron brothers arrived in 1983, they were then recruited into The Montauk Project, and subsequently used in various time travel missions by Montauk operatives. As stated before, Duncan and Edward Cameron have now assumed new bodies. Duncan Cameron still goes by the same name, but Edward Cameron is now known as Al Bielek. But don't worry yourself trying to remember all these details, as I doubt this will ever be a question on *Who Wants To Be A Millionaire?*

Preston Nichols--aware of the fact that if the future Duncan Cameron on one end of the time portal ever saw the past Duncan on the other side of the portal, this would lead to some sort of time paradox/reality shift with decidedly disastrous results--hatched a plan with some of his Montauk colleagues to sabotage the project. Of course, without the covert participation of Duncan Cameron, this whole daring plot would've never come off and we'd all probably be living in an alternative reality right now and not even know it! Whatever the case, somehow they managed to convince Duncan Cameron that the Montauk Project was coming undone, and that his help would be crucial in righting the ship that had gone astray, namely the USS Eldridge. This plan was put into effect--when on dramatic cue--one of the Montauk renegades walked up to Duncan in the Montauk Chair and whispered: "The time is now." At that precise moment, Duncan let loose a monster from his subconscious that took form and put a big wallop on the entire Montauk Project operation, bringing it to a sudden and cataclysmic end. The monstrosity in question was a big, hulking beast, "hairy, hungry, and nasty", to quote the inimitable Preston Nichols, no master of understatement. In *The Montauk Project: Experiments in Time*, Preston Nichols goes on to say that "...after the bizarre occurrences of August 12, 1983, the Montauk base was virtually emptied. The power was restored, but lights were left off with everything in disarray. Most of the personnel were eventually rounded up, debriefed and brainwashed accordingly...after the events of August 12th, the Montauk Air Force Base was abandoned. By the end of the year, there was no knowledge of anyone being on the base."

During the course of all this--before the Montauk time portal closed--Duncan Cameron, who by now had traveled back and forth in time on numerous occasions, returned to the Montauk of 1983, while his brother Edward remained in 1943. (Now, I don't quite follow all of this myself, but let's not worry too much about the details at the moment, or we'll all go mad!) At this point, it was discovered that Duncan's body was dying, and that he was rapidly aging due to his involvement in all these Montaukian time travel shenanigans. Somehow, Montauk scientists were able to copy Duncan Cameron's electromagnetic signature and transfer it to a new body. To make this operation a reality, Duncan Cameron, Sr.--a mysterious figure himself in the lore of Montauk and Naval Intelligence--was contacted by high Montauk mucky-mucks, who traveled back in time and persuaded the elder Cameron to sire a son. It was this child, Duncan Cameron Jr., who was imprinted with the electromagnetic signature of the dying Duncan Cameron from the future. So, in this case, the question begs to be asked: Who came first, the chicken or the egg? The Duncan Cameron body swap is just one more in a long line of time travel conundrums that litter the pages of the Montauk book series, and sets the reader's head a-swimming through a maze of reality shifts and time travel mind-trips. In regards to Al Bielek's body swap, Bielek states that age regression techniques were used to place Edward Cameron (that's who Al Bielek was in his previous existence) into a body in the Bielek Family. (For those of you keeping score at home, you might as well give up, 'cause it all gets even kookier from here.)

Recently, I heard Al Bielek on the *Coast To Coast AM* radio program speaking his oft repeated Montaukian mantra about how he'd been Edward Cameron in a previous life upon the USS Eldridge, as well as the standard version of the Philadelphia Experiment story as presented in the books of Preston Nichols and Peter Moon. During this program, a caller to the show stated that he--as well--has been a crewmember aboard the Eldridge during the same Philadelphia Experiment time period. The caller in question disputed Bielek's astounding claims that the USS Eldridge had been blasted straight out of the space-time continuum. In response, Bielek didn't really address the matter, but if he had, the argument no doubt presented would have been to the effect that this former crewmember had probably been brain-washed, and that his memories of the Philadelphia Experiment wiped clean by Montauk operatives, which seems to be the party line espoused by the likes of Bielek, Nichols, et al. when someone comes forth testifying to have been on the Eldridge during the Philadelphia Experiment, and that nothing out of the ordinary happened.

Another convenient argument--offered up by Montauk experiencer Glenn Pruitt--is that the reason the Montauk Project is so difficult to prove, is because it all transpired in an alternate dimension, which many observers could construe as a cop-out, because how the hell are you gonna prove an alternate dimension?? Of course, proving all these far-flung assertions is like wrestling one's way out of a Chinese finger trap: the more you struggle to make sense of this miasma of muddled mysticism, the more lost you become in a Montaukian maze.

But as much as the Montauk Mythos seems naught but a pile of happy horseshit, it continues to attract serious researchers and spiritual searchers into its endless stream of mysteries. As Montaukian investigator/experiencer Chica Bruce related to me:

> What I've come away with is that everything is true and that nothing is true...Any story (not just about Montauk - EVERY story) is ultimately irrelevant and useless to me outside of what it can teach me about Creation and the empowerment of humans via insights about how reality works. To this end, the study of the wacky world of Montauk has been extremely useful...It is cosmically humorous to me that a story so full of seemingly deranged allegations does contain many valuable, penetrating truths about consciousness and the nature of reality. The Montauk mythos is repugnant to current consensus world-views and it puts off mentalities that are fundamentally invested in conforming with the hegemony.

> Those who feel a need to bash the Montauk story are failing to understand what it is really about and are revealing their unflagging allegiance to certain stodgy mind patterns and core beliefs...

A reoccurring claim among Montauk experiencers is that advanced mind control experimentation has been perpetrated not only upon themselves, but also the local townspeople of Long Island, New Jersey, upstate New York and Connecticut, beamed from the infamous Montauk transmitter tower. This is what is more commonly known as the art and science of psychotronics, and specifically--as regards the Montauk Project--the transmission of UHF/microwave energy through the atmosphere, ostensibly bombarding the beleaguered brains of unwitting subjects, not to mention various indigenous animals-- domestic and wild--that have been reported going berserk upon occasion and running amok through the town of Montauk.

One of these Montauk Project subjects was none other than super-psychic Duncan Cameron. By using psychotronics in concert with Duncan's surreal psychic abilities, Montauk scientists were somehow able to intensify his powers vis-à-vis the creation of alternate reality vortexes. This psychotronic experimentation consisted of operating the Montauk transmitter at different pulse widths, different pulse rates, and varying frequencies. The ultimate goal behind all of these fantastic fiddlings was to see how brain waves could be entrained, whether it be controlling a super psychic like Duncan Cameron to create alternate reality vortexes used as time travel portals, or the ability to generate transmissions that could change people's moods, and cause agitation. What we're describing here could be classified as non-lethal weaponry, though I've heard disturbing reports from my colleagues in the mind control research community that microwave transmissions of a certain frequency could potentially boil someone's brain into oblivion, which certainly qualifies as something quite "lethal", as opposed to "non." The ultimate goal of all this bad craziness is total control of the human species, which apparently is what the Montauk Project was all about. Other uses for these microwave-boosted transmissions include the ability to focus on a car and stop all electrical functioning. This, of course, is the same effect commonly reported in UFO sightings attributed to alien craft, illustrating how high tech black ops can be used to replicate a so-called alien encounter. As Dr. Michael Persinger has demonstrated, certain frequencies approximate the alien abduction phenomenon. So perhaps the entire Montauk Project is exactly that: an MK-ULTRA mindphuck designed to mess with the mass mind of humankind. It has also been suggested that certain forms of electromagnetic waves can affect weather patterns. This could explain the strange summer snows that have visited the town of Montauk in past years.

One of the most vocal critics exposing the use of covert technologies of this type is Col. Tom Beardon. A former military intelligence officer, Beardon at one time published *Specula*, a magazine devoted to the study of "psychotronics" and "bio-energetics". In the mid 80's, Bill Jenkins hosted a radio program on A.M. KFI in Los Angeles, which--on a weekly basis--dealt with subjects of the paranormal. The first time I tuned into Jenkin's show his guest was none other than Col. Beardon, who spoke of a mysterious "woodpecker" signal, which during that era had become the hot topic among ham operators around the world. Beardon claimed this signal emanated from the Soviet Union which had been traced to an alleged "Tesla Generator" in the cities of Riga and Gomel, and that the "woodpecker" signal was responsible for weather modification wars covertly waged upon an unsuspecting United States citizenry by the wily and unscrupulous Russians. These manipulations of U.S. weather patterns allegedly created a drought in the western states, which in turn caused severe effects on farming and the economy in 1976, the same year the infamous "woodpecker" signal was first discovered.

It has been suggested that weather modification and mind control is the driving force behind the mysterious Project HAARP, which likewise is said to have originated from the brilliant mind of Nichola Tesla. This also falls in line with certain Montaukian mythologies, as the Montauk Project has been allegedly involved--to a certain extent--in weather modification using technology similar to both the HAARP Project, as well as Wilhelm Reich's Cloudbuster. Tesla, so states the Montauk crowd, was the main man behind the first phase of the Philadelphia Project, but later bowed out of the experiment when he witnessed its deleterious side effects, and the direction the overall project was heading. Tesla also claimed contact with aliens, and that they were responsible for passing on certain knowledge that helped with his inventions, much in the same fashion as Montauk scientists supposedly received guidance from extraterrestrials concerning the Montauk Chair.

One apparent goal of the Montauk Project was to send military operatives back in time to alter historical events, allowing the Montauk Group to hold the future hostage, and to manipulate it for their own nefarious means. (Chica Bruce refers to these exploits as "high tech Black Magic.") This notion has been seconded by Montauk experiencer Stewart Swerdlow, who--after attending a Preston Nichols lecture some years ago--experienced the sudden resurfacing of suppressed memories regarding the Montauk Project. Among other wild and woolly claims, Swerdlow says he was sent through the Montauk time portal packin' a pistol, on a mission to blow Jesus Christ to Kingdom Come. But when Jesus materialized in old town Jerusalem--and came sauntering down the steps of the temple all beatific and such--Swerdlow got cold feet and opted not to pull the trigger. (Perhaps the thought of burning in Hell for ALL eternity had something to do with his decision!) Later, Swerdlow was sent back in time again, and on the next occasion encountered Christ on the cross. On this occasion, Swerdlow was charged with the mission of extracting vials of holy blood from the crucified Messiah and, in the course of events, was apparently successful in this endeavor. The whole motivation behind this madcap Montaukian scheme was to clone the holy blood of Christ and then inject psychic superstar Duncan Cameron with it. Then--according to the Montauk Project game plan--the medical community would test Cameron's blood against the DNA residue on the Shroud of Turin, which would unanimously confirm the revelation of Christ's Second Coming. As a result of this psychic vampirism, humanity would then fall to its knees and worship this pseudo Christ, Duncan Cameron, the second only begotten Son of God! The ulterior motive behind all these blasphemies was to create the actual anti-Christ, thus ushering in a New World Order. (Now, why anyone would want to do that is beyond me!)

To mystify this matter even more, Peter Moon believes there is a strong occult connection to The Montauk Project, mainly in the form of Aleister Crowley, who Moon suggests was manipulating reality in the early part of the 20th century, traveling backward and forward in time "through a purely magical basis." The apparent reason Crowley was able to so freely time travel was due to the fact that he wasn't locked into any dimension or illusion of reality. A master of many mystical disciplines and secret schools, Crowley was able--through his Will-To-Power--to jettison himself literally through time and space, and into other dimensions, which is a really cool thing, if you think about it. But also, one must possess a very strong and disciplined intellect to be able to subject themselves to such paradigm shifting adventures without going stark, raving bonkers. Perhaps Aleister Crowley was just the man to fit the bill. Or perhaps it's all a crock of horse water...

During the summer of 1918, Crowley took a "magical retirement" to Montauk Point, the specifics of which remain obscured to this day, although Peter Moon suspects that this visit was related to the future freaky developments associated with the Montauk Project. In *Montauk Revisited: Adventures in Synchronicity*, Moon alludes to the possibility that Crowley may have been "creating worm holes from the physical realm to other realities and back again", and that the "bizarre manipulations at Montauk and in Philadelphia could have been elaborate physical deployments at the behest of simply one very powerful magician." In the opinion of one Montauk insider, Crowley is seen as a "wild joker who was romping around and having a good time without regard to how it might affect us." Moon recognizes this joker archetype as The Fool from the Tarot deck and comments that: "This is the wild creative impulse that started the whole universe. It is the force that creates will-nilly, on whim and without regard to consequences." Crowley mentions in his *Magical Diaries* that he picked up an odd colony of blisters during his stay on Montauk, and that they remained with him for five years. Whether these were attributable to some strange paranormal Montaukian event is unknown.

A former Scientologist, Peter Moon makes no bones about the vital influence he feels L. Ron Hubbard had upon these multifarious Montaukian mysteries. Hubbard was intimately involved with Crowleyan protégé Jack Parsons in a magical endeavor called The Babalon Working. According to those partial to a Montaukian worldview, Parsons--with the help of Hubbard and Parson's wife, Marjorie Cameron--succeeded in creating a fissure in the space time continuum, which was quite similar to the type of vortex associated with The Philadelphia Experiment: a doorway into another dimension. After the Babalon Working, UFO sightings began to be reported en masse, as if a Devil's Floodgate had been opened, and into the earth realm flew powers and demons from beyond, much like an H.P. Lovecraft tale, unleashed on an unsuspecting human populace.

In his Montaukian scenario, Peter Moon portrays Hubbard as a White Knight in a realm of high-tech black magicians; one of the "good guys" engaged in psychic warfare with malevolent mind controllers and rascally reality manipulators. Hubbard, it has been conjectured, was an agent of Naval Intelligence, who later claimed that he had infiltrated Parson's O.T.O. group on behalf of the U.S. Government in order to break it up. Eventually, Hubbard would apparently have a falling out with his friends in high places, and in fact found himself at war with both the CIA and IRS. Much of his disharmony with these various governmental bodies had to do with L. Ron's objection to MK-ULTRA agents bent on warping the minds of humanity. Or, at least, that's the picture Peter Moon paints within the pages of his Montauk books.

Part of L.Ron Hubbard's ontology revolved around the theory that inhabitants of Earth (that's you and me) were formerly space aliens some million billion years ago and that we are working out our complex karma here on terra firma until eventually we can arrive at that much-sought-after Scientology state of "Clear", which is likened unto "Cosmic Consciousness" in the parlance of the New Age crowd. From all appearances, certain aspects of the Montauk Project mythos seems to be a continuance of Hubbard's space opera.

Furthermore, Peter Moon suggests that there exists a certain bloodline connected to the Cameron namesake, of which Hubbard is an apparent member. Among other members of this bloodline are--as would be expected--super psychic Duncan Cameron, and his immediate family. Add to this list Jack Parson's wife, Marjorie Cameron, as well as such evil mind control geniuses as Dr. Ewen Cameron of MK-ULTRA infamy, and what we have is a genetic-Cameron-code inherently adept at such practices as magick and interdimensional travel. Moon indicates that there's an ongoing battle of good and evil taking place within the Cameron bloodline, pitting the likes of an Ewen Cameron against L. Ron Hubbard, for instance. Hubbard, it should be noted, was the only public figure to condemn the activities of Ewen Cameron during the late 60's, when Cameron was active on the MK-ULTRA front, prescribing such treatments as "psychic driving" for his "patients". Apparently, bloodlines such of these play a major role in what's going on behind the scenes with the Montauk Project, not only in regards to the Cameron connection but as well with the aforementioned Montauk Boys, who were allegedly selected for experimentation due to their unique genetic qualities.

Hitler Was A Good American:

The Bush Crime Family and a Kindler, Gentler Fascism

When Prescott Bush dug up Geronimo's skull as part of an initiatory frat-boy ritual, this ghoulish graveyard grab set in motion the first in a series of Bush Family crimes that culminated in its monstrous magnum opus, the WTC tragedy of 9/11, Dubya's very own Reichstag, where amidst the lingering smoke and ash-strewn wreckage he emerged triumphant, issuing forth a call to arms directed at an unseen menace that may be staring back at you from the mirror. But we're getting ahead of ourselves...

Pappy Prescott--after his desecration of this aforementioned sacred Indian burial site--decided his next course of action would be to align himself with the Nazi party of the 1930's. (As a side note, I've always based my selection in Presidential elections by not voting for the candidate who would look most comfortable in Nazi regalia. Needless to say, I voted against Reagan and Bush amidst these troubled visions of Gentle George and affable Uncle Ronnie dressed to the nines in SS uniforms and sporting toothbrush moustaches.) With a thousand points of light in his kinder, gentler crosshairs, Herr Bush—during his administration—brought the New World Order out of the shadows and into the beltway, throwing it full-force into the face of the American people. But once again I'm getting ahead of myself...

In the late 1980's, an FBI document surfaced demonstrating that George Bush was part of the CIA management team behind the Bay of Pigs invasion, code named "Operation Zapata". Zapata, it so happens, was the name of Bush's oil drilling company. At the time of the Bay of Pigs invasion, Bush had oil rigs located a mere thirty miles off the coast of Cuba near Cay Sal, a CIA operations base. In this regard, former CIA members have alleged that Bush allowed the CIA to use Zapata as a front for their Cuban operation, working in cahoots with several legendary spooks, including E. Howard Hunt, Frank Sturgis and Felix Rodriguez. Vice Pres Tricky Dick Nixon was also knee-deep in these covert operations directed against Castro's Cuba. These very same spooky alliances that conspired against Castro appear to have been the same players cast in leading roles in some of the most popular

126

conspiracies that have colored our generation's imagination, from the Bay of Pigs/JFK assassination through to Watergate, October Surprise, Iran-Contra, Votescam and ultimately 9/11. And the Bush Junta can be traced back to all of the above. But shit, I got ahead of myself once more...

A CIA agent named "George Bush" just happened to be in Dallas on the day that JFK got blown away, as was former Vice Pres Nixon whose purported reason for being there was to deliver a speech at a Pepsi Cola convention. *I'd like to teach the world to sing in perfect harmony*...It should be noted that Prescott Bush is credited with creating the winning Eisenhower-Nixon ticket of 1952, and in fact had cultivated a relationship with young Tricky Dicky dating back to 1941, at the same time he was courting darling Dolphie (Hitler).

In the late 1980's--when these revelations of George Bush in Dealey Plaza first came to light--CIA officials claimed that the "George Bush" in question was just some simple clerk shuffling papers, and not the very same George Herbert Walker Bush we have all come to know and love. The CIA has never been able to clearly identify this other George Bush, which only causes the plot to thicken and sicken. Of course, Bush has claimed he can't exactly remember where he was when Kennedy got his cranium catapulted across Dealey Plaza and into the history books. Go figure...

Some have suggested that Nixon's ascendancy to the Presidency was through the barrel of a gun and that the same gang of goons behind the Bay of Pigs operation were also the ones who took JFK down in one bright shining moment. During the Watergate period, George Bush was Nixon's Director of Central Intelligence (DCI). Although it has been claimed that Bush had no relationship with the CIA prior to his appointment to this post, it's hard to take this assertion seriously. With his DCI appointment, Bush ostensibly became The Company's "keeper of secrets", the biggest of which was the knowledge of the Dealey Plaza death squad. And the conspiracies keep on coming...

As the 1980's rolled around, The October Surprise featured George Sr. on a secret mission to Paris on the weekend of Oct. 18-19, 1980 to negotiate the release of the hostages in Iran, this according to former Israeli intelligence official Ari Ben-Menashe in testimony before Congress in the early 1990's. At this time, Ben-Menashe claimed that he saw Bush and William Casey at a downtown Paris hotel as they headed into a meeting with a representative of Iran's ruling faction, although Bush denied that this meeting ever took place. Whatever the case, this arms-for-hostages deal--according to the popular conspiracy theory--helped usher in the reign of Uncle Ronnie and the face of friendly fascism.

It has also been conjectured—by other "conspiracy theorists"—that Reagan was just a Howdy Dowdy type front man for the Bush Junta pajama party. Curiously enough, sonny-boy Neil Bush had dinner with Scott Hinckley, brother of John Hinckley Jr., shortly before Hinkley took pot shots at Uncle Ronnie.

So was the Bush crime family responsible for Uncle Ronnie's "attempted assassination"? (Insert creepy organ music here.) Was this, in effect, a coup de ta that put Bush at the helm of the Secret Government, leaving Reagan in place as the friendly fascist front-man ("Great Communicator") while behind the scenes Bush was calling the shots for Iran-Contra and other assorted shenanigans including the whole S&L mess co-starring sons Neil and Jeb. And while it may appear that George Bush was ousted from power by the Slick Willie revolution, this transition was in reality a seamless continuation of Bush's foreign policy, a Bush/Clinton partnership that got rolling back in the early 1980's on a Mena, Arkansas airstrip used for drug running.

And now once again we've transitioned into another Bush Presidency that some say was won by a rigged election engineered by brother Jeb. I guess I could also talk about the cozy relationship between the bin Laden and Bush families that dates back to the mid 1970's, and its possible relation to 9/11, but I think I'll save that for another time, as I'd hate to upset your dinner.

Anyway, I hope you've enjoyed this thumbnail sketch/retrospective of the Bush Family Crime Syndicate.

Seig Heil! Support family values!

Victory Day Parade (1992)

Roll out the cannons
And pump out the chests
Old uncle Adolf
Used to do it the best
The pageant of glory
The waving of flags
To celebrate the bombing
Of children in rags

I don't know how much
Us taxpayers paid
For a war undeclared
Now this gaudy parade
It seems there's better ways
Our money to spend
Then to wage wars for Exxon
For the oil men

How many more
Of this will we see?
Wars fought with smart weapons
On sanitized TV?
How many parades
Of swastikas or stars
To afford us cheap fuel
To power our cars?

So tie a yellow ribbon
Round the ol' flagpole
And toast General Schwartzkopf
Let's all rock and roll
We all can be proud
Of this football match
We won for the Gipper
So cheers, down the hatch!

The Trickster of Truths

One of the more interesting chapters in Timothy Leary's *Flashbacks* deals with the period Leary spent (after getting kicked out of Harvard) in Mexico at the isolated Hotel 'La Catalina' where he continued his LSD research, recruiting intrepid explorers there to sample his wares in the positive set and setting of tropical sand and foam. Most of the trips taken were positive and pleasant, although one funny session was recalled where some guy flipped his wig thinking himself an ape ala *Altered States*, running around the island berserking ape-like and terrorizing the native populace.

Another interesting episode from this chapter was a visit from Carlos Castaneda, a few years before Carlos penned his classic chronicles of Don Juan's shamanic teachings. It seems that Castaneda even at this time had begun his role as cosmic prankster, doing all kinds of flaky stuff and circulating false rumors about Leary as he tried--albeit unsuccessfully--to gain admission into Leary's psychedelic hotel, and into his head. But Dr. Tim was having no part of this young conservative-looking flake, whom he figured correctly was up to some sort of mysterious mental mischief.

Upon first meeting Leary, Castaneda presented himself as a Peruvian journalist named Arana. Leary, smelling a rat, politely informed Arana/Castaneda that they entertained a policy of "no visitors" at the hotel. He shook Carlos' hand and bade him farewell, sending Castaneda back with the hotel station wagon that was making a run into the village. The next day an employee of the hotel, Raphael, met Leary with a solemn expression. Raphael informed Dr. Leary that his aunt, who was a medicine women, had imparted to him on ominous story. Seems she had been visited the previous night by Arana (aka Castaneda) who was now claiming to be a professor from a big University in California. The "professor" claimed that he was a "warrior of the soul" and needed the medicine women's assistance. He said his powers were being attacked by an American (Leary) who possessed great magic that had been stolen from the Mexican Indians. Castaneda--now claiming to be a Hispanic--wanted the medicine women to help him steal these powers back, so that he could protect the

Mexican people. When all was said and done, the medicine woman was having no part of the ruse. Little did Carlos know when he approached her that many of the medicine woman's family worked at the hotel 'La Catalina'. Carlos told her that 'La Catalina' was also the name of a bad-witch women who was his enemy. In response, she informed Castaneda that Leary was a good man under her protection, and sent Carlos on his way. (The character of 'La Catalina' appears in Castaneda's first book, *The Teachings of don Juan*. In a very roundabout manner--some have said--this character was modeled after Dr. Leary.)

The next day Castaneda showed up again at the 'La Catalina', using as before the Arana alias. This time he offered Leary a gift, said to have come directly from Gordon Wasson's personal shaman, Maria Sabina. When Leary caught Castaneda in a lie concerning this so-called gift, he once again politely asked Carlos' to leave, and--after much spirited protestation--the 'young sorcerer' reluctantly acquiesced. (Arana was, in fact, Carlos' paternal name. Arana, when translated into English means: trap, snare, fib, lie, deceit, fraud, swindle or trick. So, in his native Peruvian tongue, Carlito's Arana = Charlie Trick.)

In a recent *SteamShovel Press* article, psychedelic scholar Tom Lyttle addressed the Holy Trinity Of Sixties Psychedelia: Leary, Castaneda, and R. Gordon Wasson, reflecting upon how these three seminal figures influenced and gave rise to the psychedelic anthropology that came into fashion during that era. Wasson--a much-respected New York banker--left the business world to devote his later years to the pursuit of the mysteries of the magic mushroom, traveling to Mexico where he was introduced to its wonders by the healer-shaman Maria Sabina. Sabina--according to Merilyn Tunneshende--was also an intimate of Castaneda's own don Juan Matus.

In his *SteamShovel Press* article, Lyttle notes the mercurial relationships that Leary, Castaneda, and Wasson shared, often coming into conflict with one anther over their varied views of the psychedelic experience. Wasson felt that Leary at times was naive and reckless in his grandiose proselytizations. Conversely, Leary must have felt that Wasson was a bit of a scholarly stuffed shirt. What's funny is that this is much the same way The Merry Prankster's viewed Leary once upon a trip, when the Kesey clan attempted to raid his Millbrook research facilities, and the good doctor refused to party with The Pranksters because he was too busy with some sort of scholarly psychedelic experiment. Perhaps this is the same apprehension that turned Leary off to Castaneda; the fear that he was in the company of a trickster who was cleverly involved in some sort of role playing mind game. As for Castaneda and Wasson, the two met on a couple of occasions, and afterwards exchanged several letters over the years. Throughout it all, Wasson remained skeptical of Castaneda's claims. After his initial reading of *The Teachings of don Juan*, Wasson stated that he "smelled a hoax."

Wasson and Castaneda biographer, Richard De Mille--both admirers of Castaneda's work--were equally critical of its veracity, particularly in regards to the inconsistent use of language throughout. Where the first book had don Juan speaking formal English, in the later books he frequently used English slang. The problem here is that don Juan did not speak English, and Carlos' conversations with him were transcribed from Spanish. In Castaneda's second offering, *A Separate Reality*, there are several examples of this, as there are in the third of the series, *A Journey to Ixtlan*. In that *Journey to Ixtlan* was a recapitulation of the events that transpired at the time of the first book, these inconsistencies collectively raised the collective eyebrows of both Wasson and De Mille. Such phrases as "off your rocker" "cut the guff" "lose your marbles" "shenanigans" & "the real McCoy" were liberally peppered throughout; English slang with no Spanish counterparts. One reason for this may have been the editorial constraints Castaneda was under with the University of California Press--publishers of his first book--as opposed to the freedom he exercised afterwards with Simon & Schuster, who basically gave Castaneda carte blanche control over subsequent manuscripts. Castaneda apparently used this leverage thereafter by refusing to have his work scrutinized by any of the S&S editors. De Mille, *In Castaneda's Journey*, noted these linguistic problems, and went even further into examining the chronologies of the books, once again discovering conflicts within the time frames and chain of events.

In the end, Wasson who upon first meeting Castaneda described him as "an obviously honest and serious young man," later found him to be just "a poor pilgrim lost on his way to his own Ixtlan."

A series of books by T. Lobsang Rampa came out in the late 50's, chronicling the psychic adventures of Rampa, an alleged Tibetan Yogi adept. I read the first of the series, *The Third Eye*, back in the mid 70's around the same time I first discovered Castaneda, and was effected similarly by the tales of Rampa as I was to those of don Juan. Later, as I read other books in the Rampa series--and their claims became increasingly fantastic--I began to smell a rat behind the humble trappings and simple dress of the high mountain monk. It wasn't until the later Castaneda offerings, *Tales of Power* onward, that I likewise grew skeptical of Carlos and his extravagant and ever expanding paranormal claims.

In *The Third Eye*, Rampa detailed his initiations into the mystical world of the Tibetan Monks, and the eventual and dramatic opening of his Third Eye, accomplished not only through secret initiations, but also by way of physical means, which consisted of boring a hole into his forehead with a steel instrument. Then a sliver of wood was inserted into his head, and "there was a blinding flash." Immediately afterwards, Lobsang was able to see auras. "You are now one of us, Lobsang," one of his mystical masters instructed the young lad of eight. "For the rest of your life you will see people as they are and not as they pretend to be." Thus began T. Lobsang Rampa's strange adventures into the occult.

Other phenomena imparted to the readers of *The Third Eye* consisted of a whole grab bag of paranormal phenomena such as astral projection, clairvoyance, levitation, invisibility and past life regression. One scene, which I found particularly in intriguing, recalled a group of monks, who--according to Rampa--periodically gathered together in group meditation to converse telepathically with alien beings. At one point in *The Third Eye*, the abominable snowman even made an appearance. Eventually, these books were exposed as a hoax, written by an Englishman, Cyril Henry Hoskin. Hoskin maintained this hoax through at least eighteen sequels. At best, perhaps, Rampa's books could be called an unsophisticated precursor to the Castaneda chronicles.

What makes Castaneda's accomplishments all the more impressive is the skill in which he delivers his narratives, and their believability to the reader. This believability is due either to Castaneda's sincerity, or--on the other hand--his skill as a storyteller. In the first few books (which were better than the latter) it appears at times that Castaneda's prose is clumsy and amateurish; the prose styling of a novice. But possibly this is exactly what he was trying to approximate; to deliver the impression of your average naive Joe in the street who had been propelled suddenly into the paradigm shattering domain of don Juan Matus. Harlan Ellison, a true master of SF and Fantasy, and one of its finer critics, once placed Castaneda's books among the preeminent in the genre, no small statement coming from the likes of Ellison, who is notorious for slamming anything that appears to be even slightly hackneyed or unoriginal. But that's what good writers do; they make the difficult seem simple; the unbelievable, believable.

Although the authenticity of Castaneda's books are open to question, one--after reading them--cannot deny there's something more to them than just a fantasy spun for personal profit. Even if the books contain what appear to be inconsistencies, they are told with such a tilted zen-like spin and a sense of the mysteriousness of life encountered on the road to knowledge, that it really isn't important if the events depicted therein actually transpired; it's the trip that Castaneda sends us on that counts; and what we bring back from it that really matters.

A friend of mine who attended UCLA once saw Castaneda there and said he had the look of someone who'd seen beyond the veils of normal human perception; its unstated wisdom speaking volumes from his eyes as he momentarily glanced at my friend as they passed each other on campus one day.

But who really knows what lurks behind the jester's mask...

———

What makes this subject all the more confusing are the recent condemnations of Castaneda courtesy of Merilyn Tunneshende, who reaffirms many of Carlos' claims, but at the same time testifies that he has in recent years gone astray, and in fact has himself been tricked by the master trickster of them all, don Juan. Tunneshende claims that she is also a sorceress from the same school and lineage as Castaneda, apprenticed in the Yaqui ways of knowledge by don Juan and his loco partner in crime, don Genero.

According to Tunneshende, Castaneda was banished from don Juan's world in 1980, which corresponds with the same time frame when Castaneda's work began to be called into question. Since then, asserts Tunneshende, the old Nagual (don Juan) "has blasted Carlos into a very unpleasant energetic space, and as anyone can plainly see the quality of his books deteriorated drastically afterward."

Tunneshende says she has even heard rumors that Carlos had a nervous breakdown or psychotic split as a result of being excommunicated by his former teachers, and was afterwards treated with Lithium. (At this time he was also reprimanded by UCLA for supporting the work of Florinda Donner, allegedly a member of Castaneda's witch's circle. I have spoken to others who believe that Florinda Donner is a pen name of Castaneda.) What caused this parting of ways between Carlos' and his mystical mentor, don Juan, resulted from the way that Carlo's wanted to use energy, a way that the old Nagual "found totally abhorrent." Apparently, at this time, Carlos fell under the spell of a dark sorceress named Silvio Manuel. In all fairness to Castaneda, he refuses to acknowledge these controversial claims, or even the very existence of Ms. Tunneshende, although Tunneshende alleges that she "can describe to perfection features of Carlos that I would have no way of knowing, unless I had very "CLOSE" contact with him."

The gist of Tunneshende's allegations are that Castaneda and his associates--who are involved in the Tensegrity workshops--are nothing less than psychic vampires, draining massive quantities of energy from the naive participants enrolled in their seminars. Carlos is now a slave of the aforementioned Silvio Manuel, as are all the innocents he attracts to the workshops, from whom he draws power. Their stolen power is then fed to the Spider, Silvio. Says Tunneshende: "She finishes the draining and enslaving process. She also keeps Carlos weak enough to control, energetically speaking." In the literature I've seen advertising the Tensegrity workshops, its promoters come across more like new age entrepreneurs than psychic parasites, with Castaneda fronting the act, instructing the paid participants--at $250 + a pop, no less!--in a series of T'ai chi-like movements supposedly developed by prehistoric hunter/gatherers. Apparently there is also a video soon to hit the market with Carlos performing these very movements.

So who knows what really goes on behind the scenes of this ever-widening web of intrigue? This apparent literary/psychic feud between Tunneshende and Castaneda may be just so much mushroom smoke blown from the respective medicine pipes of don Carlos and Merilyn, who--for all we know--might be working in cahoots to further muddy the waters and perpetuate the myth of Castaneda, the mysterious sorcerer.

————————

In *Carlos Castaneda, Academic Opportunism in the Psychedelic Sixties*, Jay Fikes' presents the case that Castaneda--with literary license firm in hand--borrowed the conceptual framework for his experiences from former UCLA grad students Peter Furst, Diego Delgado, and Barbara Myerhoff, then embellished upon their already somewhat imaginative and spurious field notes.

In the early 60's, Furst, Delgado and Myerhoff were observers of Huichol Indian peyote-eating rituals in Mexico. Fikes claims that the field notes taken from these rites were subsequently fictionalized to accommodate the growing psychedelic counterculture which, at that time, was just starting to bud like young cannabis tops, waiting to be sifted and inhaled by a new generation of vision/thrill seekers. Some bought into this line of academic bullshit that had been laid down--like so many tantalizing turds--by these three anthropology students; while more seasoned and critically astute researchers were able immediately to cut through the crap. (What better place to concoct fanciful stories about exotic mushrooms than in the paddies of cow pies?) If, in fact, Carlos did borrow his early ideas from these three bulldada artists, then--as psychedelic researcher Jim DeKorne suggests--he took it to another, higher level. A level convincing enough to fool casual readers, vision seekers and seasoned academics alike. For awhile, at least.

Or perhaps Carlos did meet, during his early field research, certain medicine men and shaman women who shared with the young anthropology student their magic mushrooms and sacred visions. From these supposed encounters--some suggest--Castaneda drew the composite figure of don Juan Matus, based on persons real and imagined; from true life experiences, as well as the biographies of mystics and other holy mad men.

To your humble reporter, Castaneda's early books seem to have more of a foundation based in traditional Native American culture--specifically in regards to the ritual use of peyote, and such paranormal phenomena as shapeshifting--than the later books, which come across more like acid-addled science fiction.

In his shadowy travels to South American and other unnamed environs, I'm sure that Carlos must have did his best to ingratiate himself with as many shamans and curanderos as he could shake a magic stick at. Carlos has claimed that prior to his meeting don Juan, he had no interest whatsoever in areas metaphysical and philosophical, although his former wife Margaret says that this is all they ever talked about during they're short-lived marriage, which ended several years before don Juan supposedly entered Carlos' life. Contrary to Castaneda's apparent self-made legend, his pre-don Juan days resemble someone more in search of answers and meanings to the eternal mysteries, than they do the obtuse and skeptical young anthropologist of the time as he has portrayed himself; a very staid and conservative fellow who knew nothing of matters metaphysical, and claimed to have no interest in them at all until exposed to the teachings of don Juan. This conflicts with Margaret Castaneda's portrait of a young Carlos, who spent many an idle hour attending metaphysical lectures and reading books on philosophy and the paranormal.

Certain scenes in *The Teachings of Don Juan* reverberate with a ring of truth, in that they closely parallel and echo the stories of ritual peyote use and evil shapeshifters in Native American lore. As an example, a Native American acquaintance spoke to me with great fear and reverence about a medicine man of his tribe who was known to turn himself into a half man/half wolf to spy upon his enemies, much like the character of 'La Catalina' in *The Teachings of don Juan*, who could change her appearance at will. Likewise, the peyote visions my acquaintance shared were as equally riveting, conjuring up such deeply ingrained archetypes as demons and angels, or--as don Juan called them--"foes and allies." The most important aspect of these visions were that they taught their users a lesson; a special gift one had to earn; an experience that one did not enter into lightly, because of the inherent dangers--but whose rewards were incalculable. It must have been just these types of stories--and perhaps personal experiences--from which Carlos drew his ideas and fabricated his characters; either out of whole cloth, or as partial renderings of events or persons he encountered on his own "path of heart."

Nonetheless, there is no concrete documentation that Carlos ever actually entered into the non-ordinary world of don Juan, or any other curing-shamans or curanderos. In fact, contrary evidence exists suggesting Castaneda borrowed his ideas from a variety of sources; not only from Meyeroff, Delgado and Furst, but from the likes of Gordon Wasson, Andrija Puharich and Antonin Artaud.

As the legend goes, Castaneda first met don Juan in the Summer of 1960. According to Margaret Castaneda, in 1959, "Carlos and I had read Puharich's book (*The Sacred Mushroom*) and somehow it changed us." She noted that afterwards Carlos "seemed withdrawn." Margaret asserts that at this time Carlos took a trip to "Mexico" where he was "digging for bones." It's biographer Richard De Mille's contention that the rare "bones" Castaneda spent time digging up was the actual fieldwork that Gordon and Valentina Wasson had compiled in their researches into magic mushrooms and shamanism.

In *The Sacred Mushroom*, Andrija Puharich had heaped lavish praise on Wasson's seminal work *Mushrooms, Russia and History,* a rare two volume edition published in 1957. This two volume set would have been accessible to Carlos in the UCLA Library special collection section, and this is exactly where author De Mille theoretically places our young 'warrior' in early 1960; sitting unobtrusively in a corner, ingesting the words and images of R. Gordon Wasson like so many sacred mushrooms, planting the spores of don Juan there in his mind. During this period, according to his former wife, Castaneda was also taking creative writing courses.

In an article from *Entheogen Review* entitled "Bullshit As Fertilizer In The Garden of Truth", author Jim DeKorne suggests that much of Castaneda's work is actually bullshit piled upon bullshit. DeKorne speculates that in some instances the likes of Myerhoff, Furst and Delgado, were perhaps unknowingly slung a certain amount of BS themselves by the Huichol Indians; bullshit, which later, was further embellished upon. By the time Castaneda got his hands upon these stories, yet another layer of colored coated candy had been dumped into the mixture, leaving us with three generations of delectable doo-doo.

In Furst's *Hallucinogens and Culture*, he makes reference to "peyote enemas" which is now regarded as so spurious by enthographers that it is suspected Furst was having his leg pulled by his Huichol Indian hosts: "These gringos will believe anything!" This is akin to Carlos smoking don Juan's mushroom mixture, The Little Smoke, a purported psilocybin concoction. The fact of the matter is that when smoked, psilocybin is rendered inert, thus inactive. This reminds me of the urban legend that evolved during the '60s drug counterculture involving the use of banana peels, that allegedly when dried and cooked, then smoked, would cop its users an hallucinogenic buzz. Rock crooner Donovan sang of this in *Mellow Yellow*: "Electrical banana/Gonna be a sudden craze/Electrical banana/Gonna be the very next phase!" Of course the mellow yellow banana peel craze had little more than its customary fifteen minutes of Warhoulian fame; whereas Castaneda has now enjoyed close to thirty years of success, and is probably now more popular than ever.

Andrija Puharich's *The Sacred Mushroom* comes across equally as fanciful as any thing else in the Castaneda pantheon. *The Sacred Mushroom* revolves around the bizarre experiences of Puharich, psychic Peter Hurkos and a small group of researchers who happened upon the mysterious mushroom known as Amanita Muscaria (believed by many to be the fly agaric/Soma of The Temple of Eleusis) in the late '50s at their research facilities in the eastern US. It's been quite some time since I've read this sacred manuscript, but its premise seemed to suggest that it was by no mere coincidence (read: Synchronicity) that these mystical mushrooms seemed to pop up every where this band of intrepid explorers turned, beckoning them to come taste of its forbidden fruit, thereby inducing them into the secret rites of the ancient mystery religions. Upon succumbing to the beguiling charm of this strange toadstool elixir, the group was propelled backward into ancient Egypt and other previous incarnations, not to mention being subject to various forms of paranormal high weirdness.

Another possible instance of Castaneda borrowing from other literary works can be found in a passage from *A Separate Reality* in which don Juan describes how Yaqui warriors *see the* human aura:

"A man looks like an *egg* of circulating fibers. And his arms and legs are like *luminous bristles* bursting *out in all directions*."

Compares this to a passage from a book written in 1903:

"The Human Aura is seen by the psychic observer as a *luminous* cloud, *egg*-shaped, streaked by fine lines like stiff *bristles* standing *out in all directions*."

The above quotation comes from Yogi Ramacharaka, who--as fickle fate would have it--was a pseudonymous American hack writer of bogus eastern mysticism. Is this but one, of many examples, where Castaneda has borrowed his ideas from the popular psychic literature of the time? Once during a lecture at UC Irvine in the late '60s, a student brought up these apparent similarities, and Castaneda--ever fast on his warrior-like feet--stated his belief that this was because those who later passed on the Yaqui ways of shamanism, had originally migrated from Asia when once the two land masses of the eastern and western hemispheres had been connected. According to Richard DeMille, this was just another of Castaneda's many talents, along with earning a Ph.D. in Advanced Sorcery and writing best selling novels: The ability to conjure fanciful explanations--and opportunistic embellishments--when poised with a delicate question.

Another oft cited example of supposed Castaneda chicanery comes from the aforementioned Dr.'s Myerhoff and Furst, who have since gone on to become much respected in their fields, both now heads of University Anthropology Departments. Dr. Meyeroff was an early acquaintance of Castaneda, when both were undergraduates at UCLA, together going through the various trials and tribulations associated with writing their doctoral dissertations and attempting to make their marks upon the academic world.

Myerhoff, like Castaneda, was one of a staggering five hundred anthropology students who at the time were struggling to earn advanced degrees. This shared experience--and their mutual interests in Native American shamanism and hallucinogenic drugs--created a bond between the two, which existed for many years after their initial meeting in the spring of 1966. At this time, Carlos had been writing about don Juan for many years. Dressed always in a conservative dark suit, Castaneda--'the impeccable warrior'--worked rigorously, normally eight hours a day, five days a week, stationed religiously at one of the

139

many cubicles at the UCLA Library, writing what later become known as *The Teachings of don Juan*. Mutual friends of both Myerhoff and Castaneda had been suggesting for over a year that the two should get together, hinting that they would have much to talk about. When finally they did, Myerhoff felt as if she had met a long lost blood brother, who was walking down the same path of knowledge as herself; not only in regards to their academic struggles, but as well with their mutual interest and first hand knowledge of Native American Shamanism: Carlos with his stories of don Juan, and Meyeroff's experiences with her own personal shaman, Rincon, whom she had met in the course of her field work in Mexico. During Myerhoff's and Castaneda's first meeting, the two talked for over ten hours, as Carlos amazed and delighted Myerhoff with his tales of don Juan, the mysterious Yaqui Indian sorcerer. At last she had found not only a friend with whom she could converse to on such weighty subjects, but also someone who would be able to collaborate and validate her own field data.

Later that summer, Myerhoff traveled to Guadalajara with fellow grad student Peter Furst, where they spent several days with the Huichol Indians, tape recording peyote chants and songs, and listening to allegorical stories and explanations of ritual and myth given to her by Ramon Medina. One afternoon Medina--who at the time was preparing himself to be a Huichol shaman-priest-- interrupted their daily routine with an unplanned outing into the country. As Myerhoff was later to tell it:

> Ramon led us to a steep barranca, cut by a rapid waterfall cascading perhaps a thousand feet over jagged, slippery rocks. At the edge of the fall Ramon removed his sandals and told us that this was a special place for shamans. We watched in astonishment as he proceeded to leap across the waterfall, from rock to rock, pausing frequently, his body bent forward, his arms spread out, his head thrown back, entirely birdlike, poised motionlessly on one foot. He disappeared, reemerged, leaped about, and finally achieved the other side. We outsiders were terrified and puzzled but none of the Huichols seemed all that worried.

In late August, when Myerhoff returned to UCLA, she told Carlos about Ramon Medina's amazing waterfall acrobatics.

"Oh," replied a surprised Carlos. "That's just like don Genero!" Castaneda then went on to describe don Genaro's now legendary *Separate Reality* waterfall levitations, which were strikingly similar to

Ramon's own maneuvers, though with a couple of extra added paranormal feats thrown in for effect. Don Genaro's descent of the waterfall included not only the great physical prowess exhibited by shaman-to-be, Ramon Medina, but at times it also appeared as if he were walking on water, as it rushed across the slippery rocks below. As a finale, the ever entertaining don Genaro executed a backward somersault and disappeared from the view of don Juan, Carlos and the rest of the captivated audience who had gathered at the base of the waterfall to witness his phenomenal feat. After Carlos had shared his tale of don Genero and the waterfall, Myerhoff felt instant validation for her own research. It was a much needed confirmation of the observations and interpretations that she had witnessed when Ramon traversed the magical waterfall in Guadalajara; and very much in synch with Castaneda's own interpretation of don Genaro's performance as a rite of--and initiation into--the secret world of shamanism.

In the spring of 1970 Castaneda was invited to speak at a lecture series on the ritual use of hallucinogens at the behest of Peter Furst, organizer of the event. Each shared their own recollections of shamans manifesting agility or magic on Mexican waterfalls. Furst who had witnessed Ramon Medina's demonstration along with Barbara Myerhoff in Guadalajara, shared his account, followed later by Castaneda's own description of don Genaro's acrobatic levitations. Furst found Castaneda's rendition "strikingly similar" to his own, but didn't press the issue. By this time Castaneda had become the golden boy of New Age Shamanism, so many of his claims went unchallenged. In later years, Myerhoff suspected that Castaneda had made up this version of don Genaro and the waterfall, as related in a mid 70's interview to Richard DeMille:

> **DeMille**: Even though his part of it was made up on the spot, the feeling of mutual understanding and significance remains.
>
> **Myerhoff**: Yes.
>
> **DeMille**: He must have a remarkable ability to resonate to things people tell him.
>
> **Myerhoff**: Oh, he does.
>
> **DeMille**: The stories he makes up exactly fit the person he is talking to.

Myerhoff: They're mirrors. It's happened over and over. So many people describe their conversations with Carlos, saying, "I know just what he's talking about." But each one tells you something different, something that is part of his or her own world, which Carlos has reflected. "It's all really sexual," they say, or "it's all psychological," or "mystical" or "shamanic" or whatever they're into. His allegories, the stories he tells, seem to validate everybody.

DeMille: In *Castaneda's Journey* I called Carlos a Rorschach Man, a man on whom people project their inner worlds.

Myerhoff: That's right, and the first day we met he did that with me. I was telling him about the sprinklers on the VA-hospital lawn near UCLA. They're the old-fashioned kind that send sprays whipping around, sparkling in the sun. I told him about driving down the freeway and being dazzled by the beauty of the sunlight on the whirling water, and almost feeling I was being drawn into it, and then he described it to me from above the way he had seen it as a crow, when he was flying over it.

DeMille: Right after you had said it.

Myerhoff: Yes. (Laughing)...

———

Although DeMille wasn't fooled by the Castaneda canon, he was perhaps taken in a bit by Myerhoff and associates, whose own fraudulent exploits nearly rivaled those of the master trickster himself, though lacking Castaneda's deft and slight of hand. Among the assorted acts of ethnographical and shamanic fraudulence that later came to light under academic scrutiny (remember mushrooms grow best in the dark when fed bullshit) consisted of the following:

1) A photograph claiming to depict an Indian sorcerer "flying". The sorcerer in question later turned out to be Ramon Medina in a staged photo.

2) Furst and crowd represented Ramon Medina as a sacred Huichol "singer" though such was not the case. Whereas don

142

Juan was a literary celebrity, they attempted to market Medina--in the flesh--much the same way.

3) Myerhoff recounted many tales of Medina's sexual feats and prowess with members of the opposite sex. In reality, a true Huichol shaman-healer must live a totally monogamous life.

The above are only a few of the misrepresentations and outright lies unleashed on the academic community by Myerhoff and Associates, according to Fikes. Fikes' book proved so provocative and scandalous that at one point Dr. Furst threatened to file a lawsuit for slander.

"Now," said don Adam, "I will tell you of the Two Winds, and how Carlos tried to get blown!"

During Castaneda's short stint at UC Irvine in the early 70's, he came into contact with Ramona DuVent--a Plains Indian and apprentice shaman--and her friend and fellow grad student, Marjory Dill. DuVent and Dill were going through an occult phase, and were both fascinated by Castaneda and his purported knowledge of magic and shamanic lore.

At this time, Dill was receiving special instructions from Castaneda, who had selected her to be one of his "winds". As the legend goes, a sorcerer has four wind-women, who must come to him of their own accord. In *Tales Of Power*, Carlos had found one of his "winds", but don Juan felt that alone she was not strong enough to help Castaneda "tackle his ally". Eventually, Carlos acquired his second "wind", so to speak. Biographer DeMille considered this just one in a long line of Castaneda's literary inventions, until he received a letter one day from one of these so-called "winds", namely Ramona DuVent, and this is the story she told.

One day Dill introduced DuVent to Castaneda, and the three went out for lunch. DuVent immediately impressed Carlos as a prime candidate for his sorcererial intent. He invited her to a follow up luncheon date later that week to further discuss the matter; but true to the ways of the trickster, Carlos broke their engagement at the last moment, for reasons unknown. Dill informed a confused DuVent that Carlos had more important matters to tend to than meeting a sub-apprentice for lunch. Actually, it was probably just a technique used to confuse and gain the upper hand on DuVent, in an attempt to keep her off balance, much in the same as he was dealing with "wind" number

143

one, Ms. Dill. Such was the way of Carlos' pseudo zen-like Yaqui teachings; keep forever tossing his apprentices curve balls, and questions without answers without questions.

Before long, Dill informed DuVent that she had been ceremoniously chosen to be Carlos' second "wind". DuVent was thrilled with the prospect, realizing that such a step into the realms of sorcery could help advance her greatly upon her perspective path toward shamanism and esoteric knowledge. Besides, graduate school had been rather dull up to that point, and something as mysterious and intriguing as an apprenticeship with Mr. Carlos Castaneda was an opportunity a budding shaman-ess just couldn't pass up. In any case, she'd find out if Carlos was a legitimate sorcerer, or merely blowing mushroom smoke from his posterior side. In the meantime, Dill had been preparing for her initiation. Carlos' had given her a strict regimen to follow, which consisted of living in a twig hut he had built over her, and situated in a "place of power" in the Malibu hills. Dill was further instructed that she must cut herself off from all her friends; that they were a drain of her witchly energy, of which she would need in abundance to pass her apprenticeship under Carlos. He also told Dill to get rid of her dog, on which she spent too much attention, and to refrain from sex unless it was with a sorcerer, or a sorcerer's apprentice. Casual sex, he warned her, disperses a sorcerer's power. When DuVent heard these curious demands, she immediately grew suspicious, unfamiliar with them as any rite she'd ever heard of among the Native American tradition. The deal with the dog especially concerned DuVent. She had three of her own, and was damned if she was going to give them up unless she saw a directive from Carlos' field notes that spoke directly to the subject of dog abatement. Carlos brushed off her request by saying that he was living out of his van, and that his field notes were in L.A. When Dill inquired as to when her own initiation would take place, Carlos said he would get back to her. First he had to travel to Mexico to consult further with don Juan.

Upon his return, Carlos summoned DuVent and Dill together to inform them what'd transpired during his trip. While in Mexico with don Juan, Carlos and he had consulted with the sacred mushroom as to the acceptably of Dill and DuVent for his "winds". With the aid of the Little Smoke, don Juan *saw* that Carlos had chosen wisely, wind-wise. It didn't hurt either, that they both were stone foxes--to use the vernacular of the time. This being the case, Carlos awaited further instructions from don Juan as to the nature of the initiations. After some time had passed, Carlos' two perspective winds approached him, as they had both grown impatient waiting. Carlos' seemed agitated when the matter of initiation was brought up, and explained that he had just conferred with don Juan, who had instructed him as to the exact nature of the ritual that Carlos must perform with his "winds". He explained that these rites of passage consisted of ritual intercourse. DuVent and Dill--free-swingin' liberated 70's chicks that they were--didn't bat a figurative eyelash at this suggestion, proffering a "let's get it on, then!" attitude to Carlos', who--just the opposite--seemed terrified at the prospect of performing ritual sex magick with his two would-be apprentices. When Dill asked if it was group sex in which they were to be engaged, Carlos responded in the negative, explaining that their initiations would come in the order of their acquaintance, with Dill being the first to let her wild wind blow; then next in line to spread her wings, DuVent. When at last the day of reckoning came, Carlos called Marjory Dill to let her know he was on his way over. With this, Dill hid her dog in the back room, then mentally prepared herself from the coming of Carlos. When Castaneda arrived he seemed wary of the situation. Dill tried to put him at ease, though he insisted that something felt terribly wrong. That's when the hidden dog barked, and Carlos glared at Dill reproachfully, informing her that she could never be initiated into the lofty world of sorcery if she was not even able to follow the simplest instructions. As fate would have it, neither of Carlos' two perspective "winds" were ever initiated into the sorcerer's world. In the end, they felt Carlos' had been simply blowing them gusts of particularly hot air throughout the whole ridiculous affair.

Nowadays, I've been told, Carlos surrounds himself with attractive young ladies who are affiliated with his STARFIRE/Tensegrity Workshops. For this he has received a certain amount of criticism, but I guess that comes with the territory. Just like an old rock star who can still hit the high notes or play a mean riff, Carlos is apparently drawing large crowds these days to his classes; the young and old alike--not to mention a certain amount of groupie-types--all hoping that some of his luminous charisma might rub off on them. Though Merilyn Tunneshende makes these workshops sound like some sort of mass vampiric ritual (with Vlad Carlos' sucking the psychic energy from the auras of his unwitting victim/participants) in actuality, Tensegrity-- from what I understand--is a discipline similar to t'ai chi or yoga, but with more of an emphasis on developing shamanic powers in a transformative-like process. Carlos described Tensegrity in a 1995 interview as a series of "...magical passes to keep the body at an optimum...The movements force the awareness of man to focus on the idea that we are spheres of luminosity, a conglomerate of energy fields held together by special glue." Unfortunately the interviewer failed to elicit any further explanation as to the meaning of the proceeding statement, so you're guess is as good as mine. Whatever the case may be, these workshops are bringing in mucho bucks, and if in the process they're helping a few people find their "path of heart", then more power to Carlos and his teachings.

———————

When one strips aside the specific semantics of Yaqui sorcery, what don Juan's teachings boil down to (in his bubbling brujo's cauldron) are a handful of applied techniques similar in nature to elements of various religious disciplines such as TM, Hatha Yoga, Zen Buddhism and other popular transformative practices, including lucid dreaming and don Juan's own peculiar brand of confrontational psychotherapy. Added to these more traditional religious and transformative techniques, various psi phenomena occur with frequent regularity throughout the Castaneda canon. Telepathy, astral projection, alternate dimensions, shapeshifting, psychokinesis and levitation are just a handful of the paranormal doings witnessed by Carlos while in the company of his Yaqui and Mazatec mentors, dons Juan and Genaro.

A recurrent theme don Juan constantly harped on was that Carlos-- in order to become a true "man of knowledge"--had to stop the internal dialogue of his mind. Only then could he view the world as it truly exists. When don Juan spoke of such matters--based partially on TM-like methods--his way of explaining them, and his selection of descriptive words bring to mind those of the Indian philosopher, J. Krishnamurti. Whether Castaneda lifted certain ideas and phrases directly from Krishnamurti, we can only venture to speculate, although one can be all but certain that Castaneda was quite familiar with Krishnamurti's writings, and very well may have attended some of his lectures during the late 60's and early 70's. Stopping this internal dialogue was vital to the success of don Juan's teachings, as was the necessity of "stopping the world" (as don Juan articulated it) which is the key to *seeing*. Once one had "stopped the world", another reality emerged, one that could be expressed as *non-ordinary,* though no less real than ordinary reality.

In order to instruct his apprentice to "stop the world" and *see*, don Juan enlisted the aid of various psychotropic plants, such as psilocybin, peyote and jimson weed. As don Juan explained, drugs were not always an essential component to facilitate *seeing*; but in Carlos' case they were used as almost a last resort--like a reality blasting sledgehammer-- to bash a hole through the protective psychological armoring in which he had insulated himself. In the case of other apprentices, hallucinogens were not generally needed, but Castaneda had been so conditioned to view the world in a conventional manner, he needed something to shake him up and rock his world; something to deconstruct the wall of consensus reality he had erected around himself.

After *Journey To Ixtlan*, Carlo's had reached a point where the psychotropic drugs were no longer a necessity. Carlos' graduation from these sacraments just conveniently coincided with the New Age/Mysticism deluge of the 70's, which had replaced--to a large degree--the 60's psychedelic drug experimentation, as starry-eyed initiates sought out new and less dangerous ways to expand their minds. To meet the needs of a changing mass metaphysical market, Carlo's books now delved into areas of growing popularity with New Age consumers, such as astral projection and lucid dreaming. Whether Carlos' teachings were an amalgam of concepts gleaned from others sources--with his own personal brujo brush strokes applied to the canvas for added color--he'd nonetheless discovered a wide audience ready and willing to employ these techniques, in one manner or another. During the period I had read *Tales of Power*--which deals in part with the phenomenon of astral projection--I experienced out of body experiences not unlike those described by Carlos in his book, though I don't remember which came first: *El polo, or the luminous huevos?* Were my own OBE's simply subconscious suggestions I'd planted in my mind after reading *Tales of Power*? Or conversely, were they a validation of the phenomena as described by don Carlos? I've known a wide range of people who've used the teachings of don Juan in their own lives, though normally under no formal system or set of rules. Usually it was an interpretation of Castaneda's writings translated into whatever form best suited the user/experimenter. Many were the heads I knew who did such stuff as smoke mushrooms mixed with pot then look sideways at moon-shadows in their somewhat misguided attempts at "stopping the world". Of course, what works for one urban apprentice might be a total waste of time to another. But that's the magic of Castaneda; he is--as DeMille called him---the true Rorschach Man; his words speak on many levels, and when put into effect offer a wide spectrum of results.

My vision of Castaneda at UCLA in the mid 60's is that of a frightened and insecure young man, who--as mentioned before--was searching for his way in the world, struggling with the obvious pressures of trying to earn an advanced degree. Thus his writings of don Juan, at this time, might have helped him to achieve a two-pronged purpose: 1) as a means of elevating himself eventually into the realm of advanced academics and earning his doctoral degree, and 2) as an effective means of getting in touch with his higher (truer) self, don Juan; i.e.: the eternal wisdom in us all. Was this daily act of entering into his separate reality/library cubicle and shutting himself off from the world, a means Castaneda employed for coping with academic stress? And who better to help him through these trying times than the imaginary child-like playmate and father/figure of don Juan Matus? Was this Carlos' way of growing up and coming to terms with himself?

According to a recent article in *Time* magazine, Carlos first began writing about don Juan as far back as 1956, eleven years before his first book was published, and four years before allegedly meeting his Yaqui mentor. This first unpublished manuscript was called *The Whole World Sounds Strange, Don't You Think...?* and was co-authored by someone named Alberta Greenfield. So if in reality Carlo's ever did in fact meet don Juan, than it was several years earlier than first reported. I'm sure Carlos' would argue that by dating his first encounter with don Juan in 1960, he was just protecting his teacher's identity by further obscuring the actual dates. What say, Carlos?

Don Juan--though he often shook his Yaqui head and laughed like a child at his apprentices' incessant note-taking--on more than one occasion told Carlos' that this ritual of writing he so studiously performed was part of his "path"; a means that would aid him in becoming a "man of knowledge". Does Carlos, in this instance, once again speak metaphorically through the wise old mouth of his Yaqui sage? I think first and foremost Castaneda's mission in life was to become a successful writer; a storyteller and creator of myths. And this is just what don Juan says to him, in so many words, upon occasion: "This deliberate act of notetaking (writing) will help you grow, Carlitos; like the Little Smoke, it will teach you many things."

At the end of *Tales of Power*, Don Juan and Carlo's meet on a barren Mexican plateau. Carlos at last has been fully initiated into the mysteries of sorcery, and it is here that he bids a final farewell to don Juan, and leaps into the Abyss, metaphorical though it may be. From *Tales of Power* onward, Carlos has now become a Sorcerer, though clearly still with many miles yet to travel on his own personal journey to Ixtlan; the sorcerers land of no return. Running parallel to Carlos' fictional, or allegorical, life--in the transition between *Journey to Ixtlan* and *Tales of Power*--he earned his doctoral degree. In the concrete terms of academia--and ordinary reality--Carlos had at last become a full-fledged "man of knowledge". Now he held true power with this credential in hand; his figurative magical staff. From this point forward Carlos was a certified Sorcerer (read: New Age Guru) weaving larger and more mind boggling tales with each new book-of-the-month-club selection. In one of his later literary offerings, Carlos at last openly declared his Sorcerer's status, which was perhaps the first such instance in the history of modern literature: a self made multimillionaire New Age Guru, living out his own allegorical myth in public, and in paperback; a precursor to Shirley Maclaine's own brand of New Age nonsense. Of course, this is just one way of viewing reality, as I'm sure don Juan would be apt to point out. And even though this is the direction I'm leaning--vis-à-vis don Juan as Myth--I still consider myself a bit of a fence straddler in regards to the Castaneda Controversies: On the one hand, wanting to believe the myth; though on the other, skeptical of being had by someone--who over the years-- has shown himself to be, as Jim DeKorne describes him, "a consummate trickster with subtle truths to tell." Or perhaps he is the consummate con-man, who is so good, in fact, that he has conned himself into believing his own legend, transforming his life into an allegory.

Don Juan--like other pop cultural icons--refuses to die, in the imagination of Castaneda and his readers. At one point in the saga it appears that don Juan and don Genaro have slipped through the crack between worlds, journeying to the Yaqui Sorcerer afterlife; an afterlife that just happens to exist inside a huge green dome--or something to that effect. But this is the age of the sequel, and like Spock or Superman, don Juan is resurrected in later books (in one guise or another) enabling Carlos to further expound upon the myth--and don Juan to continue with his teachings. Like Freddie Krueger, don Juan's memory is tenacious and refuses to die, so Carlos breaths life into him again and again--or hot Sonoran desert air, as the case may be. The problem many readers have with the later books (present company included) is that they pushed the limits of credulity far beyond what most of us could take seriously. As DeKorne suggests, Carlos is "analogous to the homicidal maniac who scrawls graffiti messages: "Please stop me before I kill again," on washroom walls; Castaneda's ensuing literary output seemed to be begging us to please *stop* taking him so seriously."

Selected Bibliography

Artaud, Antonin. *The Peyote Dance*. Farrar, Straus and Giroux, 1976 (1948).

Adam Gorightly

Castaneda, Carlos. *The Teachings of don Juan: A Yaqui Way of Knowledge.* University of California Press, 1968.

ibid. *A Separate Reality: Further Conversations with don Juan.* Simon and Schuster, 1971.

ibid. *Journey to Ixtlan: The Lessons of don Juan.* Simon and Schuster, 1972.

ibid. *Tales of Power.* Simon and Schuster, 1974.

ibid. *The Second Ring of Power.* Simon and Schuster, 1977.

ibid. The Eagle's Gift. Simon and Schuster, 1981.

ibid. The Power of Silence: Further Lessons of don Juan. Simon and Schuster, 1987.

ibid. The Art of Dreaming. Harper Collins, 1994.

Clare, Ray. "The Breaching of Don Juan's Teaching: A Twenty Year Review of Carlos Castaneda's The Teaching of Don Juan: A Yaqui Way of Knowledge, (1968)" in Psychedelic Monographs and Essays. (Thomas Lyttle, ed.) PM&E Publishing, 1989.

de Mille, Richard. Castaneda's Journey: The Power and the Allegory. Capra Press, 1976.

ibid. The Don Juan Papers: Further Castaneda Controversies. (Richard de Mille, ed.) Ross-Erikson, 1980.

DeKorne, Jim. "Bullshit as Fertilizer in the Garden of Truth." in The Entheogen Review, Vernal Equinox, 1995. (Jim DeKorne, ed.)

Fikes, Jay. Carlos Castaneda, Academic Opportunism in the Psychedelic Sixties. Millennia Press, 1993.

Furst, Peter T. Hallucinogens and Culture. Chandler and Sharp, 1976.

Krishnamurti, Jiddu. The Flight of the Eagle. Harper and Row, 1971.

Leary, Timothy. Flashbacks: An Autobiography. J.P. Tarcher, 1983.

Lyttle, Thomas. "Carlos Castaneda; Criticism and Conspiracies," in Popular Alienation. (Ken Thomas, ed.) Illuminet Press, 1995.

Myerhoff, Barbara G. Peyote Hunt: The Sacred Journey of the Huichol Indians. Cornell University Press, 1974.

Puharich, Andrija. The Sacred Mushroom. Doubleday, 1959.

ibid. *URI: A Journey of the Mystery of Uri Geller*. Anchor Press, 1974.

Rampa, T. Lobsang. *The Third Eye: The Autobiography of a Tibetan Lama*. Secker and Warburg, 1956.

Tunneshende, Merrilyn. "Dreaming Within the Dream." in *Magical Blend#44*. 1994.

ibid. "War of the Wizards." in *Magical Blend#48*. 1995.

Wasson, Valentina Pavlovna & R. Gordon Wasson. *Mushrooms, Russia and History*. Pantheon, 1957.

Wolfe, Tom. *The Electric Kool-Aid Acid Test*. Bantam Books,1969.

The Mind Warper Chronicles

In December of 2002, I received the following series of emails, which are easily the most stimulating spams that have yet to enter my inbox, particularly due to the fact that the spammer in question wasn't trying to sell anything, but instead was looking to acquire certain mind warping technologies that most likely don't even exist. (At least not in this space-time continuum!)

Wondering what the hell this was all about, I did a websearch on Google Newsgroups for Tomnwrr@aol.com and discovered that this was indeed a pretty wide spread spam, which had been around for at least a couple months prior to December 2002.

Anyway, to follow is the series of emails I received from this time traveling challenged individual, and my always eloquent replies penned under the pseudonymous persona I adopted for this surreal exchange, Dr. Curtis Strange. Enjoy!

> From: <cad52@earthlink.net>
> To: gorightly@hotmail.com
> Sent: Monday, December 16, 2002 8:50 PM
> Subject: DWG #52 4350a mind warper needed! jrvLpg

Hello,

If you are a reliable supplier of the below equipment I am going to need the following:

1. A mind warper generation 4 Dimensional Warp Generator # 52 4350a series wrist watch with memory adapter.

2. The special 23200 series time transducing capacitor with built in temporal displacement.

While these time pieces normally go between $5,000-$7,000 a piece, I am having a hard time finding a reliable supplier.

Teleport to me within the next 48 earth hours and I will pay $40,000 2002 US cash. Please only reply if you are reliable. Send a (SEPARATE) email to me at: Tomnwrr@aol.com

From: <gorightly@hotmail.com>
To: <Tomnwrr@aol.com>
Monday, December 16, 2002 10:45 PM
Re: DWG #52 4350a mind warper needed! jrvLpg

Dear sir or madame:

Currently we are out of stock of the below mentioned items. Just to let you know, our "mind warper generation 4 Dimensional Warp Generators" are an earlier series and do not have a memory adapter, though this certainly could be supplemented and even enhanced to a certain degree with the Kromton Brain Wave Stimulator Multiplex, which we DO currently have in stock, though in limited supply. Our version of the "23200 series time transducing capacitor with built in temporal displacement" caused major problems in the space time continuum and I do not see how, with a clear conscience, our company can allow this item on the market until someone in the current administration addresses the ongoing problem of wormholes and how they are eating away at my temporal lobe.

Best Wishes,
Dr. Curtis Strange

From: <Tomnwrr@aol.com>
To: <gorightly@hotmail.com>
Sent: Tuesday, December 17, 2002 12:00 PM
Subject: Re: Fw: DWG #52 4350a mind warper needed! jrvLpg

If you are serious on doing business please provide a phone # I may reach you at and best time to call

Thanks

Adam Gorightly

From: gorightly@hotmail.com
To: Tomnwrr@aol.com
Date: Wednesday, December 18, 2002 12:07 AM
Subject: Re: Fw: DWG #52 4350a mind warper needed! JrvLpg

Dear sir or madame:

Please first tell me what you plan to do with these items once you get them? I do not want to be held responsible for causing a polar shift!

Cordially yours,
Dr. Curtis Strange
Amalgamated Interdimensional Suppliers, Limited

From: <Tomnwrr@aol.com >
To: gorightly@hotmail.com
Sent: Monday, December 19, 2002 1:47 PM
Subject: DWG #52 4350a mind warper needed! JrvLpg

Here is my situation, and why I need these time pieces urgently: First I won't you to know my intentions would never be to change the past for others or to interfere with past events! It's wrong! I have literally come across 100s in this timeline alone who are using time travel for no good selfish finical gain and to interfere with past events!

What's even worse is that there is an agency I shall not mention here who has been using temporal displacement to change big past events and disable certain individuals to reshape the world to their liking, which will result in WW3, the major problems to come, and the death of millions.

The first piece of equipment, the time transducing capacitor is for the purpose of changing your own past, not others. It allows for you to be the programmer of your travels. I need to take control over an illegal disturbance in my timeline which has ruined my whole life and health!

First I need the time transducing capacitor to go back and have someone make sure I was never vaccinated. There was a recall on it, it has caused me many health problems, and I was an experiment to this

154

corrupt conspiracy from the beginning starting with it. The agencies famous words are: We set things right, we change them to how they should be when in essence they really are the result of great destruction and the deaths of millions, suffering of many. This so-called government conspiracy is not the government at all. It has been decided that this species will not reach the next stage of evolution. Nanobites are actually a degenerative virus(manufactured) planted in certain members of the species believed to have already made the progression into that next stage.

I must then use the mind warper dimensional warp generator to warp my mind to my former self so that I can take back my life which has been destroyed by the evil aliens. They have messed with my life and health in the worst possible way you can imagine and now I am dying of CJD which they have infected me with. I have known two others who were messed with by these same evil beings, returned to their former self, foiled there schemes and successfully taken their life's back.

There has been a major disturbance in my timeline. My father dated this women by the name of Denise whom was from a species I will not mention here. She drugged me and also has utilized mind-transducers that she slipped into my food. They are, in fact, composed of millions of nanoprobes, microscopic, intelligent machines designed to infiltrate and influence the physical and mental functions also acting as a tracer. They have done things to me and messed with my life and health in the worst possible way you can imagine, and now I am dying of CJD, Creutzfeldt-Jakob disease.

What are your intentions in the past?

I have carefully thought and planned out my actions and taken into account the consequences which could occur and believe in my heart that I have a good chance to succeed if it is done correct. That is how I have learned of these devices and everything I know, from the 2 others I met in Florida who have returned to their former self's which were also harmed by these beings. They were able to recognize and foil their schemes from happening again. My situation goes WAY beyond this CJD! This has simply been their greatest attempt to disable my mind so far.

Adam Gorightly

My plan would be very simple: When I got back in time I would simply awake one morning in panic and tell both of my parents that I had a dream from God showing me my future. As I made small predictions of what would happen over the next couple days to them and they happened they would then listen to me. Like you will be receiving a check in the mail this week for $5,000. Or you will be getting a new truck from your company this week. Then when I had their attention I would only make one by one prediction at ONLY the APPROPRIATE times to prevent the outcome of the illegal disturbance in my timeline. I also would act like myself then including social gatherings, school and everything! I would not want to send an alert to the system in any way and would only WHEN NECESSARY use my knowledge to prevent what would happen to me.

It is obvious that they were sent back to alter my destiny and change the potential I had. As a kid I was of genius intelligence, could think and see things like nobody else. Upon being drugged and exposed to these nanaprobes it all went right down the tube, when the process was interrupted they have tortured me since and now the CJD to try and destroy my thinking pattern and mind entirely. I am a fighter, and the only thing which has kept me alive from this is natural healing, a diet consisting of vegetables, fruits, nuts, grains, and seeds, 60% of my food intake raw in it's most natural form. 8 cups of fresh carrot juice per day mixed with barley green and plenty of water. It is quickly taking it's toll though. They have done much more to me as I could explain to you in my life story.

From:<gorightly@hotmail.com>
To: <Tomnwrr@aol.com>
Date: 2002/12/20 Fri AM 01:36:03 EST
Subject: Re: Fw: DWG #52 4350a mind warper needed! JrvLpg

Dear Sir or Madame,

Due to the urgency of your letter an emergency meeting was called this afternoon with the board of directors of Amalgamated Interdimensional Suppliers, Limited (AISL) to address the seriousness of your situation. Normally, when we supply the types of items you have requested, they are for the express purpose of INTERDIMENSIONAL travel as part of

156

our planet's ongoing (albeit clandestine) battle with the evil shapeshifting beings that have entered into our realm of consciousness by way of a quantum mechanical portal allegedly located in Boca Raton, Florida.

Our business practices, in these regards, have been sanctioned by the Intergalactic Federation, of which Earth is aligned, and therefore the equipment we supply on a routine basis to Earth-based INTERDIMENSIONAL travelers (engaged in this war with these shapeshifting ultradimensional scumbags!) has been approved through rigorous testing and systematic scrutiny by our finest scientists!

Time travel, though, is an entirely different subject, and the use of said equipment is this manner is expressly forbidden by the Grand Imperial Wizards of our Solar System, in conjunction with Major League Baseball. This being the case, our board of directors have decided that at this time we are unable to supply you with the mind warping items you previously requested.

Thank you for your interest,
Dr. Curtis Strange
Proprietor

The Prankster or The Manchurian Candidate?

The Strange but True Story of Kerry Thornley

Kerry Thornley was born on April 17, 1938, in Los Angeles, California. A friend who knew Thornley growing up once characterized him as a "free thinking nerd". An odd kid with odd interests, Thornley made the acquaintance of Greg Hill at CalHi School in East Whittier, with whom he soon discovered he shared similar odd interests, including a fondness for "crackpot" cults. One of their first outings together was a visit to one such cult, a flying saucer group called Understanding.

The lads also had a fondness for bowling alleys, and it was in one particular bowling alley that they discovered—or created (depending on your point of view)—the spoof religion, Discordianism.

The Bible of Discordianism, titled *The Principia Discordia*, was first published in the mid-60s and recounts a revelation experienced by Thornley and Hill, which led to the founding of the Discordian Society. As related in *The Principia Discordia*:

> Suddenly the place became devoid of light. Then an utter silence enveloped them, and a great stillness was felt. Then came a blinding flash of intense light, as though their very psyches had gone nova. Then vision returned.
>
> The two were dazed and neither moved nor spoke for several minutes. They looked around and saw that the bowlers were frozen like statues in a variety of comic positions, and that a bowling ball was steadfastly anchored to the floor only inches from the pins that it had been sent to scatter. The two looked at each other, totally unable to account for the phenomenon. The condition was one of suspension, and one noticed that the clock had stopped.
>
> There walked into the room a chimpanzee, shaggy and grey about the muzzle, yet upright to his full five feet, and poised with natural majesty. He carried a scroll and walked to the young men.
>
> "Gentlemen," he said, "why does Pickering's Moon go

158

about in reverse orbit? Gentlemen, there are nipples on your chest; do you give milk? And what, pray tell, Gentlemen, is to be done about Heisenberg's Law?" He paused. "SOMEBODY HAD TO PUT ALL OF THIS CONFUSION HERE!"

And with that he revealed the scroll. It was a diagram, like a yin-yang with a pentagon on one side and an apple on the other. And then he exploded and the two lost consciousness.

They awoke to the sound of pins clattering, and found the bowlers engaged in their game and the waitress busy making coffee. It was apparent that their experience had been private... (p. 1-2 of the fourth edition).

During the course of their divinely inspired revelation, Kerry and Greg were "born again" into their Discordian personas of Omar Khayyam Ravenhurst (Kerry) and Malaclypse the Younger (Greg).

Over the next few years, Omar and Mal spent endless hours researching the cryptic meanings behind the obscure symbol that appeared on the chimpanzee's parchment. On the fifth night following "the Revelation" Omar and Mal shared the same dream in which Eris appeared to them and declared: "I am chaos. I am the substance from which your artists and scientists build rhythms. I am the spirit with which your children and clowns laugh happy in anarchy. I am alive, and I tell you that you are free." Ensuing visions revealed to Mal and Omar that the symbol--revealed unto them via the chimp's parchment-- was called the Sacred Chao, and for further information thereof they would need to consult their pineal glands.

Discordianism--for the uninitiated--is a "spoof" religion dedicated to the worship of Eris, the Greek goddess of chaos, known in Latin as Discordia, although some would contend that Discordianism is more than a mere spoof, and is, in fact, the world's first true religion. Furthermore, the Discordian movement has been described as a Non-Prophet Irreligious Disorganization which some claim is a complicated joke disguised as a new religion. Discordians themselves contend that it's actually a new religion disguised as a complicated joke.

Thornley Meets Lee Harvey Oswald

While in high school, Thornley had been a Marine Corps reservist. After graduation in 1958, he spent a year as a journalism major at the University of Southern California. Deciding he wasn't cut out for college, Thornley elected to fulfill his active two-year duty and enlisted in the Marines. He was first stationed at El Toro Marine base in southern California, and it was here that his path crossed that of Lee Harvey Oswald. Thornley spent a total of three months with Oswald, and during this period the two engaged in lengthy conversations dealing with politics, philosophy and a shared interest in Marxism.

After his three-month stay at El Toro, Thornley was shipped overseas to Atsugi, Japan, where Oswald had been previously stationed. On his boat trip over to Japan, Thornley began working on a novel about the disillusionment of a Marine serving overseas, entitled *Idle Warriors*. The protagonist of *Idle Warriors* was named Johnny Shellburn, a composite character based on Thornley, Oswald and several other Marines. While Thornley was in Atsugi, Oswald was discharged, and soon after defected to Russia. The news of Oswald's defection caused an immediate shift in focus to *Idle Warriors*, as the lead character, Johnny Shellburn, now became based entirely on Oswald. In essence, Thornley was writing a book about Oswald three years before the Kennedy assassination!

After Thornley was discharged from the Marines, he moved to New Orleans where he met a couple of shady characters named Slim Brooks and Gary Kirstein (aka "Brother-in-law") who were involved in the New Orleans underworld, and claimed to have connections with the intelligence community. Thornley had many lengthy conversations with Kirstein and Brooks on topics ranging from philosophy and politics to espionage and criminal activities. At one point, a theoretical conversation ensued about how to kill a president; in particular, President Kennedy. Although Thornley detested Kennedy, he considered this conversation, at the time, nothing more than a morbid intellectual exercise. These conversations would come back to haunt him.

In 1964, President Lyndon Johnson formed the Warren Commission to investigate the Kennedy assassination. Thornley testified before the commission on his association with Oswald in the Marines. In 1965, Thornley published his first book, *Oswald*, which was basically an endorsement of the Warren Commission report, and examined how a person who had delved into left wing politics could evolve into a political assassin. Later that year, Thornley was contacted by Warren Report critic David Lifton, who had taken offense with his book, *Oswald*. The two arranged a meeting at Thornley's apartment in Culver City, California, where over the course of an evening Lifton presented enough evidence to cause Thornley to do a 180-degree shift in his view of the Kennedy assassination. Thornley now believed that Oswald was innocent and that there had been a conspiracy behind the assassination.

As the 1960s progressed, Thornley got involved with the burgeoning counterculture, experimented with psychedelics, joined a free love group into mate swapping called Kerista, helped organize the Griffith Park Human Be-Ins and began formulating his own philosophy called Zenarchy.

Meanwhile, New Orleans District Attorney Jim Garrison launched his JFK assassination probe, later depicted in Oliver Stone's *JFK*. Garrison contended that a cabal of rogue intelligence agents had masterminded the Kennedy assassination and that its base of operations had been the Guy Bannister Detective Agency in New Orleans. However, before Garrison was able to bring his case to trial, both Bannister and David Ferrie, another suspect in the case, mysteriously died. At that point the key suspect in the case became Clay Shaw, director of the New Orleans Trade Mart and former CIA operative.

At the same time that the Bannister operation was active, Lee Oswald had been in New Orleans involved in various communist organizations. Garrison claimed that Oswald had been directed in these activities by rabid right-winger Guy Bannister, and had been working as an infiltrator to gather information on subversive organizations for Bannister's operation. Garrison went on to theorize that Bannister had set up Oswald as a fall guy in the Kennedy assassination by creating the illusion that Oswald was a radical communist.

In early 1968, Kerry Thornley was indicted by Garrison as part of the New Orleans assassination conspiracy that had been directed, or so Garrison claimed, by elements of the CIA. The principal witness against Thornley was a self-proclaimed "witch" named Barbara Reid, who was a voodoo worker and bohemian scene maker in the French Quarter of New Orleans. Reid claimed that she had seen Oswald and Thornley together prior to the Kennedy assassination, although Thornley denied this allegation, insisting that the last time he'd been in contact with Oswald was when the two served together in the Marines.

Oddly enough, Barbara Reid had been a member of the New Orleans Branch of the Discordian Society. Reid even went so far as to claim she was the Goddess Eris herself! Whatever the case, Reid certainly brought a high degree of chaos into Kerry Thornley's life, as he was now a key suspect in the crime of the century due to her testimony.

In 1966, *The Second Oswald*, by Dr. Richard Popkin, presented the theory that there had been multiple Oswald impersonators running around New Orleans and Dallas prior to the Kennedy assassination, portraying Oswald as a loony tune communist sympathizer, with the intent of later setting him up as an assassination patsy. When Oswald was apprehended, a photo surfaced showing Oswald at his Dallas apartment, holding the rifle that allegedly killed Kennedy. When Oswald was presented with this photo, he insisted it had been doctored, and that he knew how the photographic alterations had been made. He charged: "That is not a picture of me; it is my face, but my face has been superimposed—the rest of the picture is not me at all. I've never seen it before...someone took a picture of my face and faked that photograph." This led Garrison to speculate that the photo had been fabricated by Kerry Thornley and other accomplices.

Oswald researcher John Armstrong has recently uncovered FBI documents at the National Archives which purportedly demonstrate that neighbors of Oswald had identified Thornley as a frequent visitor to Oswald's New Orleans' apartment. The problem with these witnesses, who identified Thornley by way of photographic identification, was illustrated by a series of incidents where Garrison's investigators went around showing prospective witnesses half a photograph in which Thornley appeared, informing them that the missing half was of Marina Oswald.

A *Los Angeles Free Press* staff member later identified this photo as the same one that appeared in an edition of the January 1968 *Tampa Times*, showing Kerry standing outside a courtroom after his extradition hearing with his arm around wife Cara. The negative had been flipped in the print used by Garrison's investigators, but even his most fanatical supporters had to admit it was the same photo that appeared in *The Tampa Times*. It has also been documented that Garrison investigator Harold Weisberg had photos of Thornley altered to make him appear more like Lee Harvey Oswald, which were later used to influence potential witnesses to testify against Thornley.

Thornley's other activities, his more anarchic, Discordian ones, would also be linked to Garrison. As synchronicity would have it, an early Discordian manuscript, titled *How the West Was Lost*, had been reproduced after-hours on a mimeograph machine in Garrison's office. This clandestine copying operation occurred a couple of years before the Kennedy assassination, and was the work of Greg Hill and his friend Lane Caplinger, who worked as a typist in Garrison's office. Later, Garrison theorized that the Discordian Society was a CIA front, an idea that Kerry--ever the surrealist prankster--heartily encouraged. Little did Garrison suspect that he was an unwitting dupe in this Discordian conspiracy by the covert use of his very own office mimeograph machine.

The Illuminati "Connection"

Sometime in 1968, Thornley discovered that one of Garrison's aides, Allan Chapman, believed that the JFK assassination had been the work of the Bavarian Illuminati, that ancient and fraternal order much ballyhooed by ring-wing conspiracy theorists (such as the John Birch Society) as a centuries-old secret society that was behind communism and damn near every other socialist-inspired ill then corrupting the world and "poisoning our precious bodily fluids."

In response to all of this Bavarian Illuminati paranoia, Thornley--in the midst of Garrison's probe—began sending out spurious announcements suggesting that he (Thornley) was an agent of the Bavarian Illuminati. These communiqués were sent under the auspices of the Discordian Society. The more he read about the Bavarian Illuminati, the more fascinated he became. Eventually, Kerry and his fellow Discordian conspirators started planting stories about the Discordian Society's age-old war against the Illuminati, accusing everyone under the sun of being a member of that sinister and sneaky organization, from such politicos as Nixon, LBJ, Daley, and William Buckley to Martian invaders, and various conspiracy buffs--plus members of the Discordian Society itself--which made it all very confusing and extremely hilarious.

Robert Anton Wilson--who in due time became an expert authority on the history of the Bavarian Illuminati--contributed to the formation of this Illuminati/Discordian mythos, feeding his own unique perspective and arcane knowledge into this twisted loop of conspiratorial high weirdness. What became known as "Operation Mindfuck" was in full swing by late 1968, when Wilson--in cahoots with Thornley--composed a letter and answer in the Forum section of *Playboy*, which Wilson was then editing. This spurious correspondence put forth the theory that the wave of political assassinations taking place in America had been orchestrated by the Bavarian Illuminati.

Under the auspices of "The Bavarian Illuminati," Kerry invented a Do-It-Yourself Conspiracy Kit, which included stationary containing dubious letterheads. As noted, "Omar [Thornley] would send a letter to the Christian Anti-Communist Crusade on Bavarian Illuminati stationary, saying, 'We're amused you've discovered that we've taken over the Rock Music business. But you're still so naïve. We took over the business in the 1800s. Beethoven was our first convert.'" As Wilson noted in *Cosmic Trigger*, these Illuminati/Discordian hijinks set in motion a new mythology:

> The Discordian revelations seem to have pressed a magick button. New exposes of the Illuminati began to appear everywhere, in journals ranging from the extreme Right to the ultra-Left. Some of this was definitely not coming from us Discordians. In fact, one article in the Los Angeles Free Press in 1969 consisted of a taped interview with a black phone-caller who claimed to represent the "Black Mass," an Afro-Discordian conspiracy we had never heard of. He took credit, on behalf of the Black Mass and the Discordians, for all the bombings elsewhere attributed to the Weather Underground.
>
> Other articles claimed the Illuminati definitely were a Jesuit conspiracy, a Zionist conspiracy, a banker's conspiracy, etc., and accused such worthies as FDR, J. Edgar Hoover, Lenin, Aleister Crowley, Jefferson and even Charlemagne of being members of it, whatever it was (p. 64).

In a recent interview, Wilson remembered: "I appointed myself the head of the Illuminati, which led to a lot of interesting correspondences with other heads of the Illuminati in various parts of the world. One of them threatened to sue me. I told him to resubmit his letter in FORTRAN, because my computer wouldn't accept it in English and I never heard from him again. I think that confused him." Eventually, Operation Mindfuck started to run amok, as Wilson noted in *Cosmic Trigger*: "We were all having a lot of fun with Discordianism. None of us were aware, yet, that Operation Mindfuck could get out of hand."

The Three Tramps

In the mid-1970s, revelations concerning a conspiracy of rogue intelligence agents involved in the Kennedy assassination appeared in a book by A.J. Weberman and Michael Canfield entitled *Coup d'Etat in America*. Weberman and Canfield brought to light the story of three tramps, who were picked up by Dallas police in Dealey Plaza following the assassination and released shortly afterward. The authors contended that these three tramps were actually intelligence agents in disguise who were part of a Kennedy assassination hit team.

Weberman and Canfield presented evidence indicating that one of the tramps, known as the "old man tramp," was actually E. Howard Hunt, renowned CIA agent who had been involved in various capers including the Watergate burglary and the Bay of Pigs fiasco.

When Thornley came across this evidence, he immediately recognized Hunt as the shadowy character he'd met in New Orleans over a decade before named Gary Kirstein, a.k.a. "Brother-in-law." This evidence opened up a floodgate of memories for Thornley. He began to suspect he'd been hypno-programmed as a substitute fall guy in the Kennedy assassination in the event that the Oswald set-up went awry, and that Hunt had been one of his "handlers."

If Hunt was "Brother-in-law," then who was Slim Brooks? Thornley speculated that Slim Brooks was, in reality, Jerry Milton Brooks, a former Minuteman and employee of Guy Bannister. Furthermore, Thornley suspected that Slim had acted as navigational advisor for the Bay of Pigs invasion, and had been assigned to keep an eye on Thornley during the period when he lived in New Orleans.

Only a few years prior, Thornley had considered Jim Garrison's investigation a McCarthy-like witch-hunt; now he began to suspect that Garrison might have actually been on the right track. Suddenly a string of evidence--which had once seemed but mere coincidences--were now beginning to line up, one after another, to form in his mind a conspiratorial domino row, with Thornley at center stage surrounded by a web of conspirators manipulating his movements and Lee Oswald's movements, prior to the Kennedy assassination. Thornley began sending out affidavits to friends, law enforcement officials and politicians, outlining his conversations with Kirstein and Brooks in New Orleans during the early 1960s and how he felt he had been sucked into the JFK assassination.

One day, Bob Wilson got a letter from Thornley saying: "I am the most important man on the planet--I am the only one who knows all about the Kennedy assassination!" Due to this knowledge, Thornley insisted that his life was threatened by a sinister cabal of conspirators who wanted him silenced. Wilson tried to calm down Kerry by rationalizing the situation, reminding him that there was a distinct difference between "theory" and "proof." Much to Wilson's surprise, Thornley now suspected him of being involved as part of an "assassination conspiracy team" and, furthermore, that Wilson was Thornley's CIA baby-sitter, covertly employed by the Agency to keep a watchful eye on him.

Wilson insists he and Thornley met only once, in Atlanta in 1967. As Wilson recalls: "[Kerry] had the impression that I came to Atlanta more than once and that I had given him LSD and had removed the programming the Navy had put into him when he was in the Marines-- and that I was one of his CIA handlers." When Wilson informed Thornley that he didn't remember any of this taking place, Thornley said that was because, as Wilson explained in a recent interview, "It's hard to communicate with somebody when he thinks you're a diabolical mind-control agent and you're convinced that he's a little bit paranoid."

In Thornley's worldview, Operation Mindfuck had come full circle, biting him square on the derrière. As Wilson ruminated in *Cosmic Trigger*:

> Thornley's letters to me became increasingly denunciatory. He now believed that the Discordian Society had been infiltrated very early by CIA agents (probably including me) who had used it as a cover for an assassination bureau. The logic of this was brilliant in a surrealistic, Kafkaesque sort of way. Try to picture a jury keeping a straight face when examining a conspiracy that worshipped the Goddess of Confusion, honored Emperor Norton as a saint, had a Holy Book called "How I Found Goddess and What I Did to Her After I Found Her," and featured personnel who called themselves Malaclypse the Younger, Ho Chih Zen, Mordecai the Foul, Lady L, F.A.B., Fang the Unwashed, Harold Lord Randomfactor, Onrak the Backwards, *et al*. . . .

Thanks to Thornley (as well as conspiracy researcher Mae Brussell) Bob Wilson gained the reputation as some sort of CIA super-spook, as legend grew that both he and compatriot Timothy Leary were

Illuminati ringleaders who had masterminded the Kennedy assassination dance party. Of course, Wilson found such nonsense outlandish and somewhat hilarious, as it was surrealistically reminiscent of just the type of conspiratorial hoax that he and Kerry had promulgated throughout the late 60s and early 70s. As Bob related: "Mae Brussell claimed I was an agent of the Rockefeller Conspiracy, and I confessed in a magazine called *Conspiracy Digest* that David Rockefeller came around every two weeks with gold bars to keep me well stocked . . . I thought this would help improve my credit rating, but unfortunately no one seemed to believe it, but Mae."

Paranoia or Mind Control?

Before becoming paranoid himself, Thornley had very eloquently addressed the subject of paranoia, and often parodied groups and individuals who had created elaborate conspiracy theories which mirrored their own muddled minds. Later, he became like the very people he'd parodied, such as Garrison, for instance, who seemed to accept many a half-baked theory, as long as it fit his worldview, which oddly enough included Thornley as a principal player in the crime of the century. As writer Bob Black once said to Thornley: "You used to satirize conspiracy theories; now you believe in them." To that observation, Thornley solemnly agreed.

Thornley later came to believe (as did Bob Wilson, though in a somewhat different context) that Operation Mindfuck had swung open the doors of some spooky psychic realm--a realm with a sometimes twisted sense of humor--ostensibly inviting in a whole host of mad gods and hobgoblins, no doubt encouraged by the chaotic forces invoked by Eris. As Greg Hill told an interviewer during this period: "(Kerry) has recently been in a state of extreme discord. We were talking about Eris and confusion and he said, 'You know, if I had realized that all of this was going to come *true*, I would have chosen Venus.'"

As Thornley delved ever deeper into his own conspiracies, an increasingly bizarre picture began to emerge. Initially, in the mid-70s--when these sinister figures first starting flitting in the shadows--Thornley came to the conclusion that he'd been "wired"--implanted with a mind control device--during his service in the Marines. Later, Thornley came to believe that this insidious mind zap had started much earlier, perhaps even before birth, and that he was a product, of what he termed, a "German breeding experiment"; an experiment that presumably used both him and Oswald as guinea pigs.

Thornley even came to suspect his own parents were Axis spies who had cut a deal with Nazi Occultists conducting these eugenics experiments, the ultimate purpose of which was to create a Manchurian candidate. Of course, some would suggest that Thornley feigned mind control victimization and/or mental illness to conceal his role in the Kennedy assassination twister game. Jonathan Vankin wonders, in *Conspiracies, Coverups and Crimes*:

> Is Thornley's intricately conspiratorial autobiography an elaborate mind-game he plays with himself and anyone who'll join in. Or is he really an intelligence agent, with a macabre cover story for his role in the John F. Kennedy conspiracy? Or could the story be true? Is Kerry Thornley a helpless pawn in a game beyond anyone's comprehension, who somehow figured out what has been happening to him? (p. 5-6).

Kerry once admitted that--in some surreal way--he owed everything he'd become to the ominous specter of mind control, and that it wasn't necessarily a bad thing. For good or ill, this arcane path that Kerry had been led down (or which he *believed* he'd been led down) had made him, in essence, all that he was, and had not these malevolent behind-the-scenes machinations transpired, Thornley would never have written *The Idle Warriors* and *Oswald* nor would he have led such a colorful, though complicated, life. So, in this respect, mind control had been a blessing in disguise. Or, as Thornley explained in a *SteamShovel Press* interview:

> Kerry: I harbored the conceit, up until I discovered I was a mind control subject, that I was a particularly independent thinker. And so it came to me rather hard that I owed much of my thinking and much of my independence, or what looked to me like my independence [to mind control], which was actually not independence at all. . . . I'd probably have become an Elder in the Mormon Church if I hadn't become a mind control subject--it probably would have been the most perfectly boring life you would imagine."

> Kenn Thomas: So you've been saved by mind control?

Kerry: [laughs] Yeah, right . . . not that I think it's a nice thing--it's a hideous thing for your identity to be stolen from you.

While Thornley occasionally addressed his alleged mind control in a lighthearted and/or Zen-like manner, I don't believe that his mind control revelations were total put-ons, although at times Kerry probably felt that all the metaphysical jokes he'd played on others over the years had come back to bite him.

After years to battling a rare kidney disease, Kerry Thornley died on November 28, 1998. Up until the very end, he believed that the kidney disease that led to his death was the result of a conspiracy.

Conspiratorial Recollections:

An Interview With Adam Gorightly
(New World Disorder Magazine, 2004)

Ezra Pound wrote that "the artist is the antenna of the human race." The life of Kerry Wendell Thornley certainly lends credence to that theory.

Thornley was an acquaintance of - and was writing book about - lone (sic) nut Lee Harvey Oswald long before the ritual sacrifice of the Sun King on November 22, 1963 in Dealey Plaza traumatized the nation, pioneered the mid-century counterculture revolution, experimenting with alternative religions, mysticism, consciousness expansion, and sexual liberation which are now (albeit watered-down) off-the-peg big block lifestyle choices, even prefiguring the mainstreaming of conspiracy theory in the '80s and '90s (Oliver Stone's *JFK*, *The X-Files*, Art Bell), when Thornley became convinced he was at the centre of a vast and sinister conspiracy (involving mind control brain implants and all) in the '70s.

Who better to write the biography of Kerry's obscure-nerd-kid-to-beloved-homeless-zen-schizo life than self-described "crackpot historian" Adam Gorightly, author of the Manson biography *The Shadow Over Santa Susana: Black Magic, Mind Control and Manson Family Mythos* (and the new chapbook *Death Cults*)?

We here at NWD loved *The Prankster and the Conspiracy: The Story of Kerry Thornley and How He Met Oswald and Inspired the Counterculture* and thought it would be righteous to interview Adam about his soon-to-be underground classic.

New World Disorder: So how did you get interested in such a relatively obscure character such as Kerry Thornley? Most people who have heard of Kerry most likely came across him in Robert Anton Wilson's books, but don't know much apart from the information contained in said books. Why did you think Kerry worthy of a full-length bio?

Adam Gorightly: Certainly Kerry Thornley was an obscure figure to most of mainstream America, although to those of us in the marginal fringe, he's a legendary figure; a legend that continues to grow after his death, which happened in 1998.

I became aware of Kerry in the mid 80s, when I was researching the Kennedy assassination and happened upon Kerry's curious tome, *Dreadlock Recollections*, which was a product of the zine movement. Soon I became aware of Kerry's writings in other zines, as well as his involvement with the Church of the SubGenius, not to mention the Discordian Society, a spoof religion created by Kerry and his friend Greg Hill in the late 1950s.

In 1991 or so I learned more about Kerry in Jonathan Vankin's book *Conspiracies, Cover-Ups, and Crimes*, which got into some of Kerry's conspiracies theories, one which postulated that he had been a "Nazi breeding experiment." I corresponded with Kerry during this period, and grew to appreciate the depth of his intellect, and his unique view of life. Afterwards, I started hearing some murmurings that Vankin was considering writing a bio of Kerry - which by the late 90s had failed to materialize - a book I would have ran right out and bought, 'cause I found Kerry such a fascinating figure, yet there was so much that wasn't known about him. By the late 90's, I had finished my book on Manson and was starting to put together some notes on Kerry, with vague plans of maybe writing a book someday if I could compile enough background material. Then, in late 2000, I received an email from a guy named Robert Newport, informing me of Greg Hill's passing in July of 2000.

Since I had no idea who this Newport fellow was, I responded to his e-mail, informing him that I was considering writing a book about Kerry Thornley, and was wondering if he had known Kerry, as well. Newport informed me that he'd been close friends with Kerry in high school, and had also been a founding member of The Discordian Society!

To this day, it remains a mystery as to how Newport knew to contact me at a private e-mail address - not the address I display on my website. When I later brought this up, Newport himself was unclear as to how he came to contact me. Whether by fate or dumb luck, this chance encounter was to Moses what that burning bush was. Newport held the key to the unfolding of many mysteries, which you can read all about if you buy my book!

In the same mysterious manner that Newport entered into my life, similar synchronicities continued to reveal themselves - and shit, I hadn't done any psychedelics for many a year! And so it was that each new contact led to another, and one door led to several others, and on and on. Things kept falling into my lap. Before I knew it I had embarked upon a path of no return. I plunged boldly forward, not knowing where the hell it would all end up. But I'm glad I did. I met a lot of cool people along the way - people who had known and loved Kerry Thornley, warts and all, and I learned a lot about a period of history that might have gone unnoticed if I hadn't dipped my toes into it. Life's crazy like that sometimes.

NWD: What's your take on Thornley's connection to the JFK assassination? Any validity to his mind-control conspiracy claims? Or just paranoid schizophrenia? Sometimes the most outlandish claims have a fragment of truth, bent out of shape maybe, but valid in some way.

AG: I explore many possibilities and theories in my book regarding Kerry and the Kennedy assassination, mind control and paranoia. My approach is not to draw any final conclusion to explain all the high strangeness that surrounded Kerry Thornley. Trying to make sense of it all would drive someone crazy, which was the very same maze that Kerry felt himself being sucked into. What came first: the chicken or the egg? Did Kerry go crazy due to mind control? Or was Kerry crazy to begin with, and just confabulated his role in the Kennedy assassination and as a victim of MK-ULTRA mind control experimentation?

For the record, Greg Hill thought there was something at the very core of Kerry's conspiracy theories, and that something sinister might have indeed gone down during Kerry's days in New Orleans leading up to the Kennedy assassination, and perhaps even earlier during the period he was in the Marines with Oswald, but because of Kerry's paranoia everything got blown out of proportion, and expanded way beyond what any "rational" person is able to digest. And of course there are those who suggest that Kerry made up all these wild theories to conceal his role in the Kennedy assassination by pretending to be a nut-job and thereby spreading disinformation. As with anything, there's no easy answer when it comes to Kerry Thornley. But that's what made him such an interesting character.

NWD: During the course of your research did you find that Thornley had any connections or run-ins with some of the more spookier streams of '60s culture such as Manson, the Process Church . . . Scientology?

AG: I didn't go into it too much in my book, but Barbara Reid, the principal witness in Garrison's case against Kerry, was associated with the Process Church when they were active in New Orleans in the mid-sixties. In a letter Kerry sent me in the early 90's, he mentioned dropping in to see the Process during the same period he was in New Orleans testifying to the grand jury in the Garrison case. Kerry said they gave him the creeps. Kerry also went on to say that Robert Anton Wilson had dropped acid with some of the Process members, for whatever that's worth.

As for Manson, Kerry corresponded with Charlie at one point. Apparently Manson sent Kerry a Xmas card which Kerry later auctioned off to help some homeless woman in Atlanta. It's a small world after all . . .

NWD: The book in part is dedicated to the memory of conspiracy researcher Jim Keith. Were you friends, a colleague, or just an admirer? Any thoughts on his mysterious passing? Is a Jim Keith bio next?

AG: You could call me a friend of Keith's - although we never met in the flesh. We corresponded with each other for several years. Jim and I had talked many times about getting together, unfortunately it never happened. I feel we were kindred spirits. And a number of people have compared my books to Jim's, which I consider a great honor. I try to take the same approach that Jim did with the way he treated the world of conspiracy theory in his writings. Yes, he was definitely a colleague. We shared information on many occasions and picked each other's brains. This was mainly through email correspondence. The field of conspiracy research lost a giant with his passing.

I wrote an article entitled "Jim Keith, Burning Man and 'Wounded Knee'" which appeared in a recent issue of *Steamshovel Press*. This piece entertained the possibility that Jim's death was a ritualistic sacrifice, executed by the Cryptocracy. *Steamshovel Press* editor Kenn

Thomas discusses Keith's mysterious death in an updated version of his book *The Octopus*, which was co-written with Keith. Kenn suspects that Jim's death was the result of a conspiracy. He also has a chapter on Ron Bond's death, who is the other person I dedicated *The Prankster and the Conspiracy* to. Bonds (of IllumiNet Press) was Kerry Thornley's publisher and also published many of Jim Keith's books. Kenn also suspects foul play in Ron Bonds' death.

NWD: It was weird when I read the dedication, for I was thinking about Keith at the time, partly about his book *Saucers of the Illuminati*, where Jim describes a powerful psychedelic experience he had when he was younger. I wonder how many conspiracy researchers were influenced at some point by psychedelics, whose mind-expanding qualities opened them up to other realities and novel connections? Any thoughts?

AG: Well, you certainly asked the right person that question! I don't specifically remember the passage from *Saucers of the Illuminati* where Jim talked about a psychedelic experience, but I had an interesting (to say the least!) psychedelic experience of my own when I was in my late teens. This was later recounted in an article I wrote for *Crash Collusion* magazine back in the early 90's called "UFO's, LSD and Me." This experience definitely had a profound effect on me. If I hadn't experienced it, I doubt that I'd be where I am now. And what a long, strange trip it's been!

ACKNOWLEDGEMENTS

MACK WHITE is a cartoonist, illustrator, writer, and investigative journalist whose work has appeared in Gnosis, Details, PULSE!, Heavy Metal, True West, Zero Zero, El Vibora, Strapazin, Stripburger, and many other magazines in the U.S., Japan, and Europe. He has also published four books of original stories and artwork: The Mutant Book of the Dead (Starhead Comix) and Villa of the Mysteries #1, 2, and 3 (Fantagraphics). White's research on Waco and other conspiracy topics has been published in such magazines as The Nose and FringeWare Review. He was also interviewed in the documentary "Day 51: The True Story of Waco" and has been a guest on radio talk shows across the country. Mack White may be contacted at P.O. Box 49575 / Austin, TX 78765 or at mackwhite@austin.rr.com

ASHLEIGH TALBOT'S artwork graces the cover of this compilation, as well as my first book, *The Shadow Over Santa Susana: Black Magic, Mind Control and the "Manson Family" Mythos*. Madame Talbot has a website at http://www.madametalbot.com/. Your humble author enthusiastically encourages you to navigate there and immediately purchase some of her wares. You won't be disappointed.

ERIC YORK is an illustrator, writer and musician who publishes various zines and comix, including The Hungry Maggot, Vermis Rex, Tillinghast's Moribund Fairy-Tales, and Eldritch Pulp Adventure. He currently resides in New Megiddo with his cat, Boris. Contact him at hungrymaggot@netscape.net

Digital Mac guru and co-founder of the design studio TAOpro.com, ANDREW TAYLOR divides his time between photographing the unusual, designing web sites and restoring his 1924 house in Los Angeles with his wife Michelle.

Illuminaughty Productions, Inc.

(A subsidiary of The Konformist Kollective)

CPSIA information can be obtained
at www.ICGtesting.com
Printed in the USA
BVHW051329140922
647021BV00001B/183